9 CRITICAL MISTAKES

MOST COUPLES MAKE

Dr. David Hawkins

HARVEST HOUSE PUBLISHERS

EUGENE, OREGON

Cover by Koechel Peterson & Associates, Inc., Minneapolis, Minnesota

This book includes stories in which the author has changed people's names and some details of their situations to protect their privacy.

NINE CRITICAL MISTAKES MOST COUPLES MAKE
Copyright © 2005 by David Hawkins
Published by Harvest House Publishers
Eugene, Oregon 97402
www.harvesthousepublishers.com

Library of Congress Cataloging-in-Publication Data
Hawkins, David, 1951-
    Nine critical mistakes most couples make / David Hawkins.
        p. cm.
    Includes bibliographical references.
    ISBN–13: 978-0-7369-1349-2
    ISBN–10: 0-7369-1349-1 (pbk.)
    1. Spouses—Religious life. 2. Marital conflict—Religious aspects—Christianity. I. Title.
BV4596.M3H39 2005
248.8'44—dc22   2005001515

Printed in the United States of America

05 06 07 08 09 10 11 12 / DP-MS / 10 9 8 7 6 5 4 3 2 1

This book is dedicated to the couples who have entrusted their personal lives to my counsel. They have taught me much about critical mistakes in marriage and what we can do to grow beyond them.

Acknowledgments

Writing is primarily a solitary exercise, except as I imagine you, my silent audience. Thankfully, I have a number of supportive people surrounding me who help break the isolation and offer guidance to the work. Their combined expertise and passion bring greater depth and quality to my writing. Their feedback serves to enhance what I have written, though ultimately I am responsible for the finished manuscript. I have a number of people to thank for their help with this book.

First, I feel privileged to work with the wonderful staff at Harvest House Publishers. I cannot imagine more ardent supporters than this select team. Thank you to all who work behind the scenes to bring this book to the reader.

I am grateful for the continued direction and professional guidance from my special friend and colleague, Terry Glaspey, who believed in the value of this book. He felt it was a needed topic and encouraged me to write it. Thanks again, Terry.

Gene Skinner, again, worked tirelessly as my "point man" to add strength and clarity to the manuscript. In between offering tidbits of cautious advice, always allowing for my voice, his wit and humor make for a delightful relationship. Thank you, Gene.

I cannot pass the opportunity to again thank my parents, Henry and Rose Hawkins, who smile at my books. They, along with my siblings and their spouses, encourage my writing. Though my siblings want me to write a bestselling suspense thriller, I think they are coming to accept that I must write about what I know—relationships.

I have the wonderful benefit of having two others I have mentioned in other books. What a joy to have them continue on as my primary support. Jim, a seasoned writer himself, offers his watchful eye and years of expertise, working closely with me to strengthen the manuscript. I have grown more thankful for his help with ideas and critically helpful comments.

Again, I am deeply indebted and immeasurably thankful to Christie for supporting me in my writing. She believes not only in this topic and the importance of bringing it to you, the reader, but also in my skills and passion to say it. She nudges me gently forward when I get discouraged. She catches many of the repeated errors and foibles in writing that I cannot seem to remember. Thank you, Christie, for believing in me and my work.

Finally, I never take for granted the gifts and opportunity the Lord has given me. I pray that I will be a faithful steward of them.

Contents

Chapter One

Learning from
Our Mistakes

The greater the difficulty, the greater the glory.
—CICERO

The chairlift ride to the top of the mountain was numbing. I wrapped the scarf snugly around my head and neck, hoping to shield myself from the southeast wind that bit through my stocking cap. I tucked my knees into my body and hugged myself in a futile effort to stay warm. Everyone on the chairlift was quiet, conserving energy. Except for the soft whistle of wind through the trees, the landscape was silent.

As the chairlift carried my friend Tad and me toward our landing, a gangly stand of lodgepole pine on a barren hillside just above us caught my attention. Twisted but sturdy, laden with ice and snow, the knotty conifers seemed dead at first glance. But upon closer inspection, I saw shoots of green foliage emerging.

I turned to Tad, a professional biologist, and asked how anything could possibly grow in rocky soil at 9000 feet above sea level, besieged by 30-mile-an-hour winds, encumbered by the weight of snow and ice for six months of the year.

"Look closely, David," he said. "What do you see?"

"I see trees that could use water, sunshine, and tender, loving care. They're bent and broken. They look as cold and frozen as I feel."

"Look closer."

I examined the gnarled, ruddy trees once more. Their bark was twisted and peeling in places. Several trees were literally entwined, clutching one another for dear life. I couldn't spot a single young tree.

"These trees have grown strong enough to withstand the wind, snow, and ice," Tad said. "The weaker trees have died off. Those that remain are rugged and tough. They have to be to withstand this weather. But they are here to stay."

"Sounds like this story has a moral," I said. "Stay out of the wind, or you'll freeze your tail off."

"That's a good moral for us today," Tad said. "But something else is worth noticing. Look at how the trees are grouped together. They survive partly because they don't make the critical mistake of going it alone. Isolated seedlings don't make it. They need the other trees to protect them from the brutal weather."

Tad paused for a moment, gazing at the winter landscape. "Adversity makes you strong and helps you learn what you need to do to survive and even thrive."

Marriage Is Difficult

As I reflected upon those sparse but powerful pines enduring at 9000 feet, I thought of the many married couples I have worked with over the past 28 years. Some seemed to thrive after only a brief tune-up. They came to see me for a short time and left feeling renewed and ready to enjoy their marriage once again. I have also spent countless hours with couples that struggled, digging deep to find new skills and eventually growing stronger. And sadly, I have also worked with those that have succumbed to the bitter winds of domestic turmoil and shallow soil of relational immaturity.

"Life is difficult," M. Scott Peck wrote in his popular book *The Road Less Traveled.* He could have said, "Marriage is difficult" just as truthfully. After all, marriage and relationships make up much of what we call *life.* When marriage and relating are going well, we usually do well. When marriages and relationships are in the throes of chaos, life is painful and difficult.

This is certainly not surprising information. God created us as relational beings. Bearing the image of a relational God, we long to be in partnerships with people who love us, care for us, and understand us. Alone, we may enjoy gazing at a majestic mountain peak in the shadow of a setting sun, but we treasure the experience even more when we are with someone who appreciates it as much as we do.

So what makes marriage so difficult? Why do more than half of marriages end in divorce? And why is that number no better in church populations than the general population? Let's consider a number of factors.

God Created Marriage

You will remember that in Genesis, God said that everything He created was good—except for one thing. He said that for man to be alone was not good. God created the stars and galaxies. He created every kind of animal. He created cool, clear streams and magnificent mountain peaks, and He placed man in the midst of this verdant paradise. Then, from the very companionable side of man, He took "bone of my bones and flesh of my flesh." God made a helpmate for man to ease the pain of his loneliness and to provide a fulfilling relationship.

When we look at the heavens and consider how all of creation fits together like a giant jigsaw puzzle, we sense an unseen hand behind it all. God's design is miraculous. But closer inspection reveals an important caveat. God gave man and woman free will. Adam and Eve—and by extension, you and I—chose to disobey God. Ruling a handmade paradise was not enough for us. No, we wanted more—we wanted to be like God. One of the consequences of that decision is that we no longer live in peaceful harmony with the earth or with one another. Having succumbed to our selfish, sinful nature, we act in ways that create havoc in our society and in our marriages.

As we review the circumstances of Garden living, we note that after man and woman chose to disobey God, they did a number of things we still do today. These behaviors are at the root of many relational mistakes we will consider in this book. Note Adam and Eve's behaviors in the Garden:

- They flirted with the temptation to become like God.

- They disobeyed God.

- They hid from God.

- They felt shame and self-consciousness.

- They blamed someone else for their problems.

- They experienced problems in their immediate family relationships.

These behaviors started at the very beginning of humankind and continue to this day. They are the primary culprits in marital problems. As you read through this book, you will see that many thorny problems in marriage grow from these roots.

What's So Critical?

So, what makes a mistake a *critical mistake*?

We make mistakes every day, especially in marriages. But not all mistakes are *critical mistakes*. What is the difference? Larry makes a mistake when he forgets that his wife has been struggling with her boss at work and needs extra TLC in the evenings. He makes a *critical mistake* when he habitually fails to champion his bride when she is under stress. He is consistently caught up in his own business dealings and no longer listens to his wife as she shares her burdens. She eventually feels unappreciated and disconnected from her partner.

Perhaps an example from my own counseling practice will illustrate the point. Jerry works long hours as an engineer and feels stressed much of the time. He is a no-nonsense person at work and brings that attitude home in the evenings. He has an irritable edge that Barbara, his wife, does not appreciate. When they fight, things spiral out of control quickly. Arguing occasionally is not wrong. Being irritable once in a while is not a mistake. But when minor skirmishes constantly evolve into World War III, something is wrong. When domestic tension becomes a way of life, the problem is critical.

Mistakes happen, and marriage partners need tolerance for one another's occasional foibles. But when the errors become habitual and occur in one of the nine critical areas we will outline in this book, a couple needs help. A marriage will not last long or attain a high level of quality if one or more of these critical mistakes exists in a relationship.

Difficulties Are Predictable

Men and women have quarreled since the beginning of time. Rest assured that Adam and Eve did not always have peace in the home—at least not after the apple incident. Can you imagine this scene?

> "Hey, Adam. Would you mind helping me prune these trees?"
>
> "Yeah, I'll help you in a while. Right now I want to go hunting."
>
> "Can't it wait? I need your help."
>
> "Are you kidding? A big herd of buffalo is coming through the valley this week. If I miss this run, we may have to go without meat this winter. Do you want us to risk starving because the fruit trees need trimming?"

Eve grumbles as she walks away, turning to shoot Adam one last sneer. Adam and Eve had their problems. The same is true for married couples throughout time.

But lest we stop there and feel helpless in the face of tension, disharmony, conflict, and the ever-present threat of divorce, we should also acknowledge a powerful truth: Conflict is predictable, and we can manage it. The conflicts we face have patterns, so we can learn—with God's help—to overcome these problems. We can learn from our mistakes.

Like Adam and Eve, we have developed the fine art of hiding, avoiding, and blaming. We have learned to make mountains out of molehills and molehills out of mountains. We have found ways to avoid learning the incredibly helpful lessons available to us in every squabble we face. But because our relational problems are predictable, we can learn new strategies to overcome them.

Paul and Linda

Paul and Linda were typical of many couples that have come to see me. They had struggled with marriage problems for years before they finally decided they needed outside help—a difficult step for them to take, they said.

"Our problems are trivial in many ways," Linda told me. "We should be able to solve them ourselves, but we can't. We both figured we needed to get help."

Married for 18 years with two adolescent children, Paul and Linda had allowed confusion and anger to erode some of their affection for one another. Now those things threatened their marriage.

Paul was a tall, friendly man, a fireman by trade. He told me he enjoyed his work, but more importantly, he enjoyed the time off from work when he could pursue his passion—fishing. Linda was a thin, athletic woman who worked as a nurse at the local hospital, enjoyed the challenge of an occasional triathlon, and actively followed their daughters' extracurricular activities.

I asked them what had brought them to counseling.

"We keep fighting over the same issues," Linda said. "Every time I think things are improving, we go back into a spiral of arguing and bickering."

"It really is nothing big," Paul added, "just the same old patterns that send us into fighting and make us angry with one another for days. It's stupid."

"Most couples fight about the same things over and over again," I said. "They don't recognize their patterns or the implications of them, so they never work their way out of them."

"That's us," Paul said, looking over at Linda. "Sound familiar?" he said to her.

"We have two or three issues that seem tŏ trip us up," she said. "We keep fighting about money and how to discipline the kids. Otherwise, we get along great."

Paul leaned over to Linda and took her hand. She seemed to like his touch. I could see their relationship had a lot of warmth, and yet if they could not identify their destructive patterns and eliminate or minimize them, their marriage would be in trouble.

As if reading my mind, Linda jumped in. "We don't want to let things get to the point where the fights tear us apart. We both believe our marriage is worth saving. We hope you can help us see the patterns and change them."

I worked with Paul and Linda for the next three months. The emotional warmth I saw between them that initial afternoon faded at times as we explored their areas of disagreement. Paul was reluctant to face issues head-on and was clearly more comfortable playing the clown than confronting problems. Meanwhile, Linda tended to blow things out of proportion and was overly sensitive. But both showed a willingness to stick with it, look for destructive patterns, and change them.

Even though Linda and Paul were motivated, change was not easy. Real change never is. The situation was especially difficult for Paul. He was unaccustomed to sitting down and talking about problems. He worked with men who considered attending counseling and discussing personal problems to be frivolous.

Like his friends, Paul had a habit of making sarcastic comments when he was frustrated. That was his way of reducing his anxiety. Paul's sarcasm was very detrimental. And, of course, kept him from convincing Linda that he was seriously committed to solving their problems. As Paul gradually stopped the incessant and inappropriate joking, he learned to express himself without sarcasm. Not surprisingly, Linda's respect for him grew.

Linda had her own work to do. She needed to avoid exaggerating their problems or twisting Paul's words. Like Paul, she also had to change her tone of voice if they were to make progress with their relationship. She learned not to fall back on biting language when things were not going her way. Instead, she spoke calmly and remained focused on the issue at hand. This helped Paul because he was able to tune in to what she was saying rather than tuning out her bitter words. Gradually, Paul became more serious while Linda tempered her intensity. These compromises had a huge impact on their marriage as both husband and wife became more effective problem solvers.

They found that they could learn a lot from mistakes they had been repeating in their marriage. They found out that marriage can be a place where you sand off the rough edges of your personality and grow up, once and for all.

The Lessons in Mistakes

Thankfully, we can learn valuable lessons from our mistakes. Though the process can be painful, if we are sincere about the search, we will find things that help us become better people and better spouses. If we are willing to face ourselves and our problems, we will discover things that we would rather not see. But simply identifying them can be immensely helpful. Let's consider some of the things we will be talking about in *Nine Critical Mistakes Most Couples Make*.

First, *mistakes are humbling*. Relational mistakes create turmoil. They highlight your role in causing problems for another person. Unless you are hardened and insensitive, you will notice that someone hurts—and that you have caused the hurting. If you are willing to learn, your relational mistakes will bring your head out of the clouds and back to earth. In honest reflection, you will have the opportunity to see yourself more accurately—and humbly.

Second, *mistakes provide opportunities for emotional growth*. When you honestly listen to your spouse's appraisal, you will have the opportunity to mature. Your spouse will undoubtedly be willing to offer you feedback that can be immensely helpful, provided you are willing to listen.

Charles Manz, author of *The Power of Failure*, tells us that we can be liberated when we admit personal shortcomings. He used King David as an example—specifically, David's affair with Bathsheba and the murder of her husband. He also cites contemporary examples, such as President Clinton's affairs and President Nixon's Watergate cover-up. Until these people faced their failures, they were unable to move forward in life.

Manz says, "We need to face that we have failed. Until we do, we can find ourselves sinking deeper and deeper into darkness tied to the past rather than rising toward a brighter future. Our long-term success may well depend on our accepting, in the short run, when failure is really failure."[1]

Third, *mistakes teach us what is important*. We have not gone far enough when we only admit our mistakes or even try to remedy them. We must look deeply into our actions for the root problems. Saying you are sorry, as worthy an action as that is, falls short of what you can accomplish. When you review mistakes critically, you can learn about your hidden motives and values. If these are askew, you must address them.

Many couples struggle with the same critical mistakes over and over again. Perhaps that is your current situation. You may feel like the traveler who repeatedly slips into the same pothole in the road. Once you have truly *learned,* you will choose a different road. But you must first understand and accept the lessons the situation provides.

Fourth, *mistakes can be a way that God communicates with us.* He uses them to get our attention. When things are flowing smoothly in our lives, we are tempted to become self-righteous and ignore God. He allows troubles to come into our lives to increase our reliance on Him.

God also utilizes cause and effect. He allows us to experience the natural consequences of the way we have lived our lives. Let me offer an example.

Kathy was a 53-year-old professional woman who came for counseling to find help for her relationship with Tom. They were engaged, but Kathy had some lingering doubts about their relationship. Because she had two previous failed marriages, she was particularly gun-shy. She was also not particularly insightful and was the victim of patterns she vaguely understood but desperately wanted to avoid repeating.

In counseling, Kathy discovered her severe codependency traits. She latched onto men with severe emotional problems—including addictions—and reinforced their weaknesses by ignoring or catering to them. She knew that these troubled men needed her and, because of her insecurity and feelings of inferiority, selected them to both lean on and have them lean on her. Her marriages were cases of two needy people finding each other. Unfortunately, such relationships are almost always doomed to failure.

Kathy shared that Tom was a professional and worked in an accounting office with her. He was a likeable, Christian man. They had met at church and then began to date. However, after several months, Kathy discovered that Tom was a not-so-recovering alcoholic. He minimized his drinking, and she was inclined to gloss it over as well. But past experience and her Spirit-guided radar warned her of problems ahead unless they faced these issues directly. Kathy not only needed to address Tom's issues with alcohol but her own issues with codependency. If she could do that, she would make fewer mistakes in the future, thus giving her a better chance to find happiness in her relationships.

Finally, *mistakes can be fun*. Yes, you read correctly. Mistakes, given the right frame of mind, can be interesting, intriguing, and even enjoyable. Making mistakes is a part of life and relational living. Mistakes *will* happen. It is not a matter of *if* you are going to make a mistake, but *when*. Fortunately, mistakes can be instructive and actually enjoyable, if you view them in that light.

Consider how intrigued you would be if you were to stand back after making a mistake and ask yourself, *I wonder why I did that?* or *What was I thinking?* Or perhaps even *What can I learn from that non-sensical move?*

I teach couples to understand their typical relational mistakes and then be on the lookout for them. I encourage couples to take a playful stance toward their mistakes. Couples can remain in good spirits by using phrases like these:

- "Uh-oh, here we go again."
- "Are you getting the same warning signs I'm getting?"
- "Can we slow this thing down? I'm getting that nervous feeling again."

If couples can agree ahead of time to catch each other as they approach "mistake area," they can begin the change process. They will have successfully accomplished a *pattern interruption.* Interrupting the old pattern will break the cause-effect connection and create the beginnings of a new, healthier pattern.

Nine Critical Mistakes

Many mistakes are instructional, but some are critical. If habitual, they can erode affection and destroy the integrity of your relationship. I have found nine mistakes to be especially devastating to a marriage, and we will address one in each of the following chapters.

1. *Stop pushing the plunger.* In this chapter, we will learn about the importance of resolving a conflict before it takes a hazardous downward turn, creating irreparable damage. Most couples know within the first minute or two of a discussion whether it is going to be constructive or if it has the potential to evolve into all-out war. We must learn to tell the difference and make decisions accordingly.

2. *Stop whistling Dixie.* Here we will explore the danger of making molehills out of mountains, hoping that problems will disappear if we ignore them long enough. This doesn't work, and we will learn how to tackle this issue.

3. *Stop speaking Greek.* We will learn how to put a stop to obscure, distracting communication. We will learn the importance of staying focused and finding solutions to problems.

4. *Stop trying to play God.* In this chapter we slay a sacred cow—the desire within all of us to play God by telling our partners what they are doing wrong, why it is wrong, and what they should be doing differently. This seems to be a favorite pastime for many couples, but it is very destructive.

5. *Stop kicking a dead horse.* Many couples do not know when to put an issue to rest. Memories of past wrongs they have suffered

are deeply engrained, and they feel a need to remind their spouse of them whenever the opportunity arises.

6. *Stop living in the trenches.* Everyone needs a cheerleader, and the best possible choice is your spouse. In this chapter, we will examine the damage that occurs when too much criticism, or perhaps the lack of a positive attitude, clouds our judgment. We will also discuss the transformation that praise and positive regard can bring.

7. *Stop using that untamed tongue.* This chapter explores the importance of reducing criticism in your marriage. We will explore how carelessness—especially verbal carelessness—can destroy a marriage.

8. *Stop living with paper fences.* In this chapter we address the importance of healthy boundaries. We will talk about what boundaries are, why they are important, and how you can reinforce them for the benefit of your marriage.

9. *Stop being distant.* Many couples seem to fear intimacy. They may complain about their lack of closeness, but they seem paralyzed to do anything about it. We will look at what intimacy is, what barriers to intimacy are most common, and how you can take down those barriers and create warmth in your relationship again.

The Heart of Conflict

As we approach these vital issues, we must always strive to deal with the heart of the matter. Superficial change will bring frustration. Short-term solutions and quick-fix schemes are destined to failure.

Jesus provides something to think about regarding conflict and our hearts. Consider this story from His life.

A young man approached Jesus and asked Him to settle an inheritance dispute with his brother. Jesus answered him, "'Man, who appointed me a judge or an arbiter between you?' Then he said to them, 'Watch out! Be on your guard against all kinds of greed; a man's life does not consist in the abundance of his possessions'" (Luke 12:14-15).

At first glance, you would think the Lord would be willing to help a man who was asking for assistance. Why would He rebuke this man and send him on his way? Perhaps the answer lies in the last part of the passage. Listen to my paraphrase of His words:

"This is not simply a matter of making a fair distribution of your wealth. It is a matter of the heart. Instead of being myopically concerned about equality, try learning about your heart and making a fair decision based on heart principles."

James 4:1-3 highlights the heart's central role in conflicts:

> What causes fights and quarrels among you? Don't they come from your desires that battle within you? You want something but don't get it. You kill and covet, but you cannot have what you want. You quarrel and fight. You do not have, because you do not ask God. When you ask, you do not receive, because you ask with wrong motives, that you may spend what you have on your pleasures.

Does that passage hit you between the eyes as it does me? Can you trace your relational struggles to selfish motives and problems of the heart?

Instead of passionately focusing on everything your partner has done wrong or things you believe he or she ought to do to make things right, consider what is going on in your heart. Before pointing the finger at your spouse, make sure you have diligently examined yourself for any tentacles of greed. Make sure that resentment is not at work in your motives. Specifically, watch out for signs like these:

- a sense of entitlement

- a desire turned into a demand

- a gnawing sense of resentment

- a desire to get even

- a self-righteous sense of judgment

These attitudes are natural. I have had them myself and wrestle with them often. In fact, never have I felt complete victory over them. How about you? How's your heart?

A Decision to Change

You have most likely picked up this book because you have been making some mistakes in your marriage and want to break free from the troubling patterns. You can do it. With God's help and a willing heart, you can move beyond these problematic patterns into a more joyful relationship. The question is, what will you have to do to change?

First, *change requires a clear, committed decision*. Perhaps this seems obvious. But not everyone is willing to do what is necessary to effect real change. In fact, many people who say they want to change have both feet planted firmly in cement. They are not going to make adjustments regardless of what they say. Change comes from a decision to engage in transformation. That decision sets everything else in motion.

Second, *change requires a willingness to change.* Once you have decided to change, you must examine your heart to see if you are really willing. You will need to look at various areas of your life and marriage and confirm that you are ready to alter your behavior. This is *surrender*—surrender to the powerful work of God. If your marriage is not working, you must be willing to do something about it.

Third, *change requires honesty.* You cannot change what you have not faced. If you have not labeled something as a problem, you are not likely to resolve it. Therefore, before any change can occur, you must be brutally honest with yourself, acknowledging that a problem exists and that you are at least partially responsible for it. You must be willing to admit that your life and marriage are not working the way they could. Humbling? Yes. Freeing? Absolutely.

Fourth, *change requires courage.* Now that you have admitted that your life and marriage are not what they could be and that your critical mistakes are ruining your shot at intimacy, you must have the courage to change. Change is not for the fainthearted. It requires gut-wrenching bravery.

Fifth, *change requires sound judgment.* For transformation to occur, you must examine your life with sound judgment. Many say they are willing to change but have not truly counted the cost. As members of Alcoholics Anonymous say, "Half-measures availeth us nothing." Superficial change is worth little. For real results, you must acknowledge what is not working and be willing to adjust.

Sixth, *change requires perseverance.* Real change does not happen in one fell swoop. It takes resolve. It takes looking at your pattern of critical mistakes, again and again, and working your plan for change. This is part of counting the cost. If you are willing to change, you are willing to stay the course for as long as it takes.

Seventh, *change requires God's help.* We must understand that we cannot change under our own power. Albert Einstein once said that we cannot repair a problem using the same force that created it. That's why our faulty thinking—the same thinking that created the problem—is inadequate to truly remedy the problem. We need God's help.

Don't Forget to Smile

As we embark on this journey, remember that everyone makes

mistakes. Especially those of us who are married. Blunders are part of the territory.

We can hold it together with friends we see on occasion. We like our friends and want them to like us. Consequently, we often go to great lengths to put on our best face.

The same seems to be true for our relationships at church, where we share an unspoken expectation that we will be pious. We want to act like we have been listening to the sermons and are practicing the honorable Christian life. Most of us know how to look good, sitting reverently in the pew, halo barely perceptible. Sadly, we often confuse acting self-righteously with being righteous.

But behind closed doors, in the shadows of home, we let down our guard. The ongoing grind of relating takes its toll. We lose our temper, pout, and perhaps even yell. We struggle with the demons of addiction. We are, above all, human, and so critical mistakes happen. But that can change!

As we make this journey together, let's remember that we are all fallible. We all have difficulty with one or more of the critical mistakes we will address in this book. So relax. Smile. Look for yourself in the stories that follow. But whatever you do, don't take yourself too seriously. We are, after all, in process. We cannot expect to have this thing called *relating* down pat.

Chapter Two

Stop Pushing the Plunger:
Avoiding Emotional Explosions

It's never too late—in fiction or in life—to revise.
—NANCY THAYER

I clambered up the three flights of stairs to my office, clutching my morning latte for dear life. My lunch in the other hand and briefcase slung over my shoulder, I was gearing up for my first appointment. I said a short prayer for protection and a blessing for those I would see in my psychology practice that day.

"Good morning, ladies," I said cheerfully to my office manager, Helen, and her assistant, Darby.

"Good morning, Dr. H.," both said happily.

I glanced out into the waiting room. A couple sitting together, busily filling out forms, exchanged glances and chatted brightly.

"Is that my first appointment?" I asked Helen.

"Yes. The folder is ready, and they have just about finished filling out the intake form. They seem like a nice couple."

I headed back to my office to prepare for the couple waiting to see me. I wondered what might have brought them here. Maybe they were having stepfamily issues. Or they might be newlyweds, already struggling to keep their relationship intact. Perhaps one had been unfaithful, and they would ask me to help them put the pieces of their marriage back together again.

Although I call myself a child and family psychologist—kind of like the family doctor of yesteryear—marriage counseling comprises the bulk of my work. I meet with countless couples that are barely able to keep their love relationship alive.

I have seen the pattern so many times: The love-struck pair envisions a life of happiness and bliss—and then reality bites. Conflict enters the picture, and they have more on their hands than they can manage. They are often ill equipped to handle the problems that many couples face, and they come to me for help. Sometimes they try to make it alone and end up watching helplessly as their marriage dissolves.

As I have worked with couples during my 28 years of counseling, I have learned the patterns of most relational conflicts. I have come to understand that the majority of marital problems fall under one of the nine critical mistakes we will explore in this book.

In the words of an old saying, the situation is hopeless but not serious. You can learn how to prevent your relationship from falling victim to one of the nine critical mistakes. Or if some damage has already been done, you can learn strategies to help find solutions quickly so that you can more fully enjoy your relationship.

What would this couple bring on this Monday morning? They looked cheerful enough in the waiting room. Perhaps they had blended-family issues, and their struggles were with ex-spouses, not with each other. Perhaps they were trying to decide how to parent a young child. Perhaps they had been fighting all weekend and were simply putting on a good show in public. Which of the critical mistakes were they making? I would find out soon enough.

After taking off my jacket and putting my briefcase away, I went back out to the secretarial office to review the intake forms. I picked up the file and gestured to the couple, indicating I would be with them shortly.

Barbara and Thomas Simms. Both 38 years old. He worked as an assistant manager at a local department store. She was a bank teller. On the intake form, they summarized their problem like this: "We don't know how to fight fair."

Not a lot of information for me to go on but important nonetheless. Although we may wish fighting were not part of a marriage, that is obviously not the case. The couple that does not know how to fight fair is already at a disadvantage when it comes to making their marriage work.

Conflict will come. Knowing how to navigate conflict can make or break a marriage. It is one of the most powerful skills a couple must learn in order to make their relationship thrive.

I greeted the Simmses and escorted them to my office. Both gave me a generous handshake and a broad smile as they entered the room. They were certainly friendly enough.

"Hello, folks. I know we don't give you a lot of room on our forms to talk about what brought you here, so why don't you go ahead and tell me how I might be able to help."

Barbara was casually dressed in blue jeans and a sweater. Short brown hair hung softly on her shoulders. She had an engaging smile. Thomas was a tall, slender, athletic-looking man with prematurely thinning, gray hair. He wore a closely groomed goatee and was comfortably dressed in a long-sleeve oxford shirt and khakis. He was friendly but a bit more cautious in his demeanor.

After some hesitation, Barbara said, "I don't know exactly where to start."

"Well, why don't you tell me why you decided to seek counseling? What was happening in your marriage that led you to come in?"

During the next 20 minutes, Barbara and Thomas told of their 14-year marriage and their history of conflict. They smiled often at one another. They spoke calmly, their voices hardly indicative of any deeper issues. They reminisced about the strengths in their relationship—they enjoyed their work, the home they had designed and built together, and their three children.

When the topic shifted, things began to heat up. I could feel the mounting tension in the room as Barbara spoke of a friendship Thomas had at work with one his female associates, and her concern about it.

Within moments, the atmosphere turned dark with frustration and an undercurrent of hostility. Voice tones sharpened. Their words were filled with ridicule and accusation. The couple that had spoken so calmly before now began crumbling in the face of their problems.

"He always defends her," Barbara said. "He spends more time at work than at home. He cares more about his job and his special friend than his family."

"There you go," Thomas countered. "Making accusations that aren't true. Always on the attack. Never understanding my side of things."

"Well, how do you explain the lunches you two have had together in the past couple of months, and the gift you bought her for her birthday?"

"Business. All of it was because we work together, nothing more," Thomas said sharply.

"Whoa!" I said. "You guys were so friendly a minute ago, and now you're attacking one another like sworn enemies." But attempts to intervene went nowhere.

Barbara jumped in, leaning forward in her chair, directing her blunt words at Thomas.

"He doesn't care how I feel about his relationship with his sales associate. He defends himself, but I think there is something going on."

"This is nuts," Thomas said, glaring at her. "I keep a professional relationship with all my associates. We talk about this at home, but nothing I say reassures Barbara. She starts to attack me every time this subject comes up. She attacks my staff, and when I defend them, she turns psycho on me. Nothing I say can help, and I'm sick of it."

"Folks, stop it," I said. "I'm willing to help you try to sort things out and find a solution, but first you need to quit attacking each other. That won't solve anything."

They continued to glower at one another while I considered my next steps. I have seen just about everything in my years of practice, but the mood had shifted so suddenly that I was taken off guard. They had been affable one moment, chatting away and touching each other with affection. Then suddenly, they pushed the plunger, detonating emotional dynamite and sending tons of relational debris flying in every direction. Why? More importantly, what could we do about it?

The Dramatic Shift

Friends one moment, enemies the next. Lovers with hopes and dreams one moment, combatants ready for a separation the next.

Have you ever felt that way? Have you basked in the affection and friendship of marriage and then, without warning, found yourself trapped in a nasty encounter? If so, I'm not surprised. It happens, even in the best relationships, with lovers engaged to be married and with those who have been married for 30 years.

These dramatic shifts are the stuff that turns blissful marriages down a dead-end street. They can change a lovely, harmonious attachment into a bitter, argumentative rivalry. And they can happen fast enough to make your head spin.

Let's consider exactly how this occurs.

First, *someone changes the emotional rapport*. The shift can happen drastically, sometimes without anyone's awareness. Someone raises a tender topic and bruises another person's feelings, violating a temperamental ego.

Notice that Barbara and Thomas were doing well as long as they avoided "the hot topic." I discovered that they did fine when talking about the kids, finances, summer vacation, and intimacy. But when Barbara brought up the taboo topic, the emotional forecast changed from balmy and mild to torrential rains with hurricane-force winds.

Dr. Alan Loy McGinnis, in his best-selling book *The Friendship Factor*, speaks about the importance of maintaining the emotional climate in a relationship. He explains that every person brings a certain emotional energy. It can be a positive energy, as when two friends meet one another, or—in the case of a marital squabble or a sudden shift in temperament—negative energy. One person, bringing a destructive tone to the relationship, can set the stage for the other to react in kind.

Second, *defensiveness increases the hostility.* Dealing with issues in the here and now, fighting today's fights with today's energies is hard enough. But on top of that, we all carry emotional baggage into a marriage.

Before you get defensive, understand that no one had a perfect childhood. All of us grew up with circumstances that left us feeling abandoned, insecure, or unlovable. We all have "triggers" that our partners can pull. We know that we are "reactive" if our emotions about an issue exceed what we might expect for that issue.

Harville Hendrix, in his book *Getting the Love You Want*, says we carry little parents around in our heads. He says we put the face of our parents on our partner. Other psychologists have called this *transference*—attributing something to our partner that really belongs to our parents. Needless to say, this process can wreak havoc with relationships. Responding emotionally to old situations and placing them in the current one is confusing and creates emotional overreactions. We must all do our own emotional work, getting clear about whose issues belong to whom and keeping them out of our marriages.[1]

Third, *egos get bruised*. When we face a threat (or a *perceived* threat), we often shift into fight-or-flight mode. When someone assaults something we hold dear—such as our ego—something inside of us urges us to attack or flee. Men are especially good at this. Our first instinct is to destroy the threat or run from it. We rarely consider less drastic options.

Our pasts play a large part in determining how we handle present difficulties. We learned from our parents how to handle conflict. After watching our parents duke it out verbally, we may be inclined to use some of those same tactics. Or after seeing and hearing so much conflict at home, we may avoid conflict like the plague.

As I examined Barbara's history, I saw that her past was affecting her current relationship with Thomas—although Thomas certainly needed to change some of his own actions. Barbara explained that her parents had separated when she was ten. Throughout the ordeal, she was drawn into their intense conflict. As the oldest of three children, Barbara became her mother's confidant. She received all the nasty details of her father's supposed affair. Barbara's mother repeatedly told her that her father was a no-good philanderer who could never be trusted and insisted that their marital problems were entirely his fault.

Barbara's parents often used her as a pawn in their fights. Her mother expected her to side with her—without question. Barbara's mother attacked her father viciously. Although Barbara loved her father deeply, she had listened to her mother's constant tales of betrayal for far too long. As a result, Barbara was not sure what was true and what wasn't.

Today, many years after the divorce, Barbara's mother continues to harbor a great deal of bitterness and resentment toward Barbara's father. But even worse is the effect the divorce had on Barbara.

Barbara now recognizes that she felt helpless to protect her younger siblings from the verbal violence that raged in the home. In addition, because of the suspicions about her father's infidelity, Barbara is unable to fully trust the men she has become acquainted with. She fears they will eventually cheat on her, regardless of their assurances of faith. Barbara realizes that she has taken on a great deal of her mother's negativity and she may not be evaluating people and events accurately because of what transpired in her past.

Internationally recognized conflict-resolution consultant James Creighton, author of *How Loving Couples Fight*, says, "The belief that our feelings are caused by external events is not the whole truth. It is only one piece of the puzzle. The emotions you experience are created by the meanings you attribute to these events. You decide what each event means to you."[2]

I recall a recent event that completely befuddled me. I was having a conversation with a close friend of mine. We were talking about something innocuous one moment, and two minutes later I was ready to scream. The conversation went something like this:

> Christie: "David, would you mention to your son that I'd like my house painted, if he still wants the work?"
> David: "What do you mean, if he still wants the work?"
> Christie: "Just what I said. If he still wants the job."
> David: "Why wouldn't he want the job? I told you he wanted to paint your house."
> Christie: "Why are you getting so defensive?"
> David: "Because of the way you said that. Why wouldn't he still want the work?"
> Christie: "I just wasn't sure he still wanted to take on this project. He changes his mind about things sometimes."

David: "He doesn't change his mind about things like this."

Christie: "Do you hear how you are talking to me?"

David: "Well, I don't like the implication that my son will waffle on this agreement."

Christie: "I was not implying that he would waffle."

David: "Okay. Sorry. I misunderstood what you were saying. Sorry for getting so upset."

Notice how quickly I was ready to fight. I became petty, argumentative, and defensive. I was overly protective of my son and identified too closely with him. Fortunately, I had the presence of mind to note how I was behaving and end it there.

In the past, I have not always made such wise decisions. At other times in my life—far more than I would like to admit—I have taken on the role of the demanding perfectionist. I have lashed out, even when doing so was not in my best interest or the best interest of those with whom I was attempting to communicate.

Fourth, *we hurl insults to protect our egos.* Once the war has begun, anything is fair game.

As sad as this reality is, each of us has likely been part of it. We have quit caring for some people because we felt defensive or threatened. We shifted from loving concern to attack mode. We had been hurt, so we wanted to inflict hurt. We felt betrayed, so we were willing to betray.

Fifth, *at some point we declare a truce.* After the battle has been fought, someone decides this warfare between lovers is madness. Someone has to stop the emotional bloodshed and wave the white flag.

But too often, we declare the truce only after we have wounded each other's feelings. Sometimes the wounds never heal. Words cannot be taken back. Insults find their mark, and the pain can last a lifetime.

If you recognize this pattern in yourself, I hope you are ready to do the work necessary to alter it. Reading this book is a powerful beginning to changing long-standing, destructive patterns. In these pages, you will learn how to make this adjustment more quickly and effectively.

The Dynamite Effect

Recently, I drove by a newly excavated site in Washington's Cascade Range. Having seen the area a few days earlier, I wasn't sure I was in the same place when I returned. Shocked, I pulled over to the side of the road to take a closer look. Gone were the giant conifers and sprawling maples, the salal and huckleberry and sword ferns. In their place, huge earthmoving machines carved the barren landscape.

Before the heavy equipment arrived on the construction site, however, something had to prepare the earth so that it could be moved. Workers used dynamite to loosen and remove large amounts of dirt and rock in preparation for a road that was to be built through this mountainous country. In one swift stroke, someone pushed the plunger, triggering an explosion that ripped the ground apart.

I wondered about the person controlling the plunger. How did he feel as the push of a lever scarred so much life? Did he realize that the ravaged earth would never be the same?

Likewise, I wonder about those who decide to push the plunger in a marriage. Do they realize the damage they are doing? They focus on an immediate goal—to make a point, to win an argument—but do they consider the long-term consequences of their actions? Do they realize they cannot take back the words they have spoken in anger?

Just as the effects of dynamite are sudden and catastrophic, so are the effects of the tongue. I have noticed that many people seem adept at setting catastrophic actions in motion with a single word. With that one word, an avalanche of destruction disrupts communication and stirs up conflict.

The Power of the Plunger

People push the plunger for many reasons. One of the reasons—perhaps one that we do not want to look at often enough—is to gain power. The plunger controls a lot of power.

Just as workers feel powerful when they push the plunger that spews tons of earth in every direction, so people feel powerful when they push the plunger of conflict that propels words and emotions in every direction. Although most of us say we loathe these moments, perhaps we also secretly enjoy the control that accompanies them.

Let's revisit Thomas and Barbara. Let's look at their situation again from the perspective of power.

Both Thomas and Barbara wielded huge amounts of power in their earlier conversation with me. Meaningful interaction ended when they began to talk about the friendship Thomas had at work. They stopped listening and went on the attack.

Barbara felt the power that came from accusing Thomas of something ugly. She was sure that he was having an affair, and nothing would convince her otherwise. Thomas, feeling his own sense of indignation and power, defended himself vigorously. He called his wife a "psycho" and attacked her as forcefully as she had attacked him.

Notice the power at work in this encounter. Notice the *position* that each person took. Notice the defensiveness. Defensiveness, common in so many relationships, says, "You're wrong. I don't want to listen to what you have to say. I want to have my way. Just shut up."

But defensiveness and power plays do not work. Using power to defeat your opponents is not productive. You may silence them, but you do not create a space for love. Power plays drive all the love and goodwill from the relationship.

James talks about power when he says, "Those conflicts and disputes among you, where do they come from? Do they not come from your cravings that are at war within you? You want something and do not have it; so you commit murder" (James 4:1-2 NRSV).

Yes, we all commit murder when we use our power to defeat our spouses. We murder their spirits. We murder their esteem. We want to have our way because of our cravings for power, and we are willing to use words to annihilate our partners in order to get it.

The Blame Game

Another way to use our power in a marriage is to blame our partner. Each of us is familiar with this strategy. We point the finger of blame everywhere except at ourselves.

Barbara accuses Thomas of cheating on her. Thomas says that Barbara is out of her mind. Both develop rationales for their positions and then hold fast to them. They are like dogs with a bone, their teeth firmly set in place. Even with no meat left on the bone, they will not give it up for anything.

When they take their positions and the adrenaline is surging, Thomas and Barbara—or perhaps you and your spouse—cannot look at the issue from other perspectives. When we are angry, emotionally reactive, and powerfully indignant, we cannot perform certain functions:

- listening to what is being asked of you
- listening for what is not being said
- owning your part in the struggle
- listening to what might be triggered in you

Fixing blame may appear to be an attempt to solve a problem, but it is never effective. In another noteworthy book, *Don't Go Away Mad,* author James Creighton writes this:

> The need to affix blame nearly always begins with fear and self-judgment, the same attributes which plague the defensive person. At its most basic level, this behavior is an effort to dispel anxieties that really belong way back in childhood. The crazy-making part is that it has nothing to do with problem-solving, though it can seduce us into believing that it does.[3]

For a long time I clung to the belief that blaming others was a way of genuinely trying to end conflict. I remember a conflict I had with another student years ago in graduate school. We had been friends for some time and were working on an important project together. Feeling a bit of panic as we approached crunch time, I began taking responsibility for meeting our deadline. Before long, I also began to feel a growing sense of anger because I was doing the majority of the work. For weeks I brooded about the problem. As my resentment continued to grow, I knew I had to confront him. I put together a case that, from my perspective, convincingly proved I was carrying far too much of the load.

Finally, with guns loaded, I decided the time for a showdown had come. I was so convinced of my position that I sincerely believed he would have no way to rebut it. I presented my case—in a less than diplomatic manner. To my complete shock, he responded with an equal dose of resentment. I listened incredulously as I heard what I considered to be his badly skewed argument in support of his opinion.

As we exchanged accusations, the tension increased. Neither of us had harbored a clue that the other was feeling used and bitter.

Only after we launched our attacks and our harsh words had done their damage were we able to sort through the incredible misunderstanding. I learned memorable and painful lessons about blame, misperception, and resentment. Once I cooled down, I began to see that my feelings had been clouded by my underlying feelings of fear concerning the project and by a considerable degree of self-doubt about my ability to handle my responsibilities. In the end, I felt foolish and embarrassed. I had made the mistake of thinking that blaming someone else was a solution to my problem.

Creighton shoots a hole in that belief! Blame, he says, is just another futile power play. Another way of avoiding the real issues. Another waste of energy that could be used to solve the real problems.

Power that Deepens Intimacy

If blame does not work, what can we do? If blame is divisive and a waste of energy, how can we redirect those pent-up feelings in a productive way?

Creighton shows how we can use power for the sake of intimacy. What if, instead of warring against your partner, you each used your energy and power to fight a common enemy—the problem? Creighton highlights two constructive uses of power in a relationship.

Getting It on the Table

The first is to *urge the other person to acknowledge both people's emotions and deal with issues that are of importance to both.* Creighton says, "It is entirely appropriate to use your influence or power to insist that your emotions be acknowledged, that important issues be addressed, and that a resolution be sought. Bear in mind that there is a difference between these goals and insisting on a particular resolution that may give you an advantage."[4]

When resolving disputes within large corporations, this is called "getting it on the table." It requires a clarification of the issues.

I encourage couples to objectify the problem rather than attack the other person. I press upon them the importance of clarifying the *real* issue. I also insist that they recognize that people have a right to their own point of view. Even partners do not have to agree or think alike. Getting beyond this is difficult for many couples.

When one person threatens or compels the other to surrender, the imbalance of power results in a win-lose situation. Coming out on top may seem like a victory at the moment, but goodwill and trust are lost, and before long the marriage will be in serious trouble.

Intimidation is never helpful, but both partners should express their legitimate needs and emotions. Martyrdom has no room in a healthy relationship. When pleasing others is hurting you (the title of a recent book of mine), you are in trouble. Unless you bring your true thoughts and desires to the table, you will end up feeling resentful and misunderstood.

A Fair Process

Creighton explains that the second way to use legitimate power is *to insist on a process that is fair to both people.* Creighton explains that both people must have access to the same information and the same opportunity to influence the outcome.

For example, a spouse is using an unfair process when he or she uses his or her family to gang up on the other person. Using intimidation or shame to make the other person agree is not a fair process. When you use power responsibly, you state what you feel, think, and want, and you allow—even encourage—your spouse to do the same.

How would Thomas and Barbara's situation look if they had followed these guidelines?

 ☞ Instead of arguing with one another about whether or not

Thomas was having an affair, they would agree to create an environment where she trusted him.

✳ ✍ Instead of Thomas becoming defensive and calling Barbara names, he would acknowledge her feelings, attack their common enemy—distrust—and help her look for solutions.

✳ ✍ Both Thomas and Barbara would share their feelings, asking each other for what they needed without fear of reprisal and without blaming each other.

✳ ✍ Instead of using gross generalizations such as "always" and "never," they would be careful to make accurate statements that reflected how they saw things.

✳ ✍ They would do a better job of agreeing on the real issue at hand and staying on the topic.

✳ ✍ Instead of losing their tempers and launching into tirades against the other, they would agree to take a time-out when things became too heated.

✳ ✍ They would acknowledge their differences and their right to have them.

Fair-fight guidelines are almost always difficult to follow. No one wants to be reasonable in the heat of the moment. We prefer to push the plunger and let the debris fly. But in the aftermath, we regret our actions and the words we said in haste.

What Is Predictable Is Preventable

Even with the best guidelines, conflict happens—unruly, unmanageable, nasty, terrible conflict. Too often, we throw caution to the wind and push the plunger. Just remember that if you take that route, you need to be prepared to accept the consequences. And they won't be pretty!

For a more productive approach, try out some new tools. Consider that because conflict is predictable, it is also preventable. By observing how you and your spouse fight, you can change the outcome.

That's right. Watch for the patterns in your conflicts. Go through the list of critical mistakes couples make, marking those that fit you and your spouse, and agree to change them. After you and your beloved have mapped out your particular patterns, you will be ready to practice a very powerful technique called *pattern interruption*. The purpose of this technique is to alter the pattern. How you alter it is not as important as actually doing it.

For example, if your pattern is to push the plunger, agree with your spouse that you will take an immediate time-out before talking about an emotional topic. If your spouse usually pushes the plunger, ask him or her to accompany you to a different part of the house before continuing with the discussion. Perhaps you and your spouse would do well to say a short prayer before having any conversation you know will be "hot." A particularly useful verse to review at these moments is Ephesians 4:29: "Do not let any unwholesome talk come out of your mouths, but only what is helpful for building others up according to their needs, that it may benefit those who listen."

As a counselor, I find this passage to be pivotal. In fact, it might be the most helpful bit of advice on the topic of communication that I have ever encountered, especially as it pertains to pushing the plunger. If couples will adhere to Paul's counsel, it can literally spin the direction of a relationship from disaster to delight.

Consider what might happen if Barbara and Thomas only used words that were wholesome, beneficial, and edifying. What might happen if they eradicated harmful words from their vocabularies? Thomas certainly would not engage in name-calling, nor would he assail Barbara in any way. Likewise, Barbara would never lash out with unjust accusations and would instead limit her focus to those things that would strengthen—rather than harm—their relationship. Both would guard against using words that have no purpose other than to attack and destroy.

Barbara and Thomas had some very difficult work to do. They had to interrupt ineffective patterns they had learned from their parents. They practiced slowing down the pace of their arguments and listening carefully to one another's feelings. They worked on catching themselves when they blew their problems out of proportion, using generalizations to describe each other's actions. They practiced not pushing the plunger. Eventually, they were able to find solutions that worked for both of them. Thomas altered his schedule so that Barbara would not be jealous. He shared more of his work life so that Barbara was aware of what was happening there. Meanwhile, Barbara practiced trusting Thomas as his behavior changed.

What worked for Barbara and Thomas may not work for you. No single recipe works for everyone. The key is being willing to try something new. Notice the destructive patterns and work to change them. Experiment with different constructive tools, and you will surely find one that works for you.

But what if you are the only one reading this book? Is the situation hopeless? Of course not. Just remember that the only person you can change is you, so why not start there? Why not adjust how you interact with your spouse and see what happens?

As you notice the patterns, examine your part in the problems. Watch to see if you push the plunger and identify what triggers your move. Also, observe how you react when your spouse pushes it. Then change your response.

Try On Patience

Why do we push the plunger? Actually, that question has many answers. Ultimately, however, we do it because, as James says, we want our way. We become consumed with our own power, wanting what we want, when we want it. How dare anyone stand in our way? We demand to be understood. We demand that others agree with us. Yes, we *demand.*

But instead of demanding and impatiently pushing your agenda, what if you practiced patience? What if you prayed for God to change your heart so that you were gracious with those whom you love the most? What if you asked God to help you understand your spouse's heart? What if you prayed for, and practiced, the fruit of the Spirit?

Consider what the apostle Paul said. Instead of "works of the flesh," which included "enmities, strife, jealousy, anger, quarrels, dissensions, factions," what if we practiced the opposite? "By contrast, the fruit of the Spirit is love, joy, peace, patience, kindness, generosity, faithfulness, gentleness, and self-control. There is no law against such things" (Galatians 5:19-22).

Instead of pushing the plunger, consider praying for patience, and the fruit of the Spirit will surely come to you.

Consider asking God to show you what you are like to live with. To open your eyes to the qualities you bring to your marriage and to open your heart to strategies for improving them. You are only half of the equation, but you are *one* half, and positive change can begin with you.

Chapter Three

Stop Whistling Dixie:
Avoiding Problems Can Hurt Your Marriage

And I will ask the Father, and He will give you another
Counselor to be with you forever—the Spirit of truth.
—JOHN 14:16

So you've decided not to push the plunger. The destruction that occurs when one or both partners detonate emotional explosives is obvious. The sting that results from sarcasm, name-calling, and other horrible habits takes a toll that people are not likely to quickly forget or forgive. Although you may feel that momentary, sweet feeling of revenge when you lash out against your mate, you know that you will eventually have a terrible mop-up job on your hands. The destruction is simply not worth the cost.

But what about the destructive power of a habit on the opposite end of the spectrum? Instead of making mountains out of molehills, some people make molehills out of mountains. This critical mistake is akin to hearing the tromping of elephants in the room but insisting that it is merely distant thunder. Ignoring problems can be as destructive to a marriage as blowing minor conflicts out of proportion. Take a look.

Gene and Shirley seemed like a very nice couple. They came to their initial appointment holding hands and smiling warmly. He was a robust man who wore cowboy boots, a bright silver belt buckle, and a long-sleeve Western shirt. The only thing missing from his ensemble was the hat. His handshake and greeting were generous. His demeanor carried none of the reluctance most men bring to their first counseling session.

Shirley was equally warm and friendly. She was modestly built, with blond hair down to her shoulders and a short skirt. Her red lipstick matched her fingernails.

Gene and Shirley were both on their second marriage. Their intake sheet noted they were having "a few small problems" they wanted to work on. Their first marriages had been lengthy, ending when their spouses left them for someone else. Filled with bitterness and distrust, both remained single for many years until meeting each other at their church's singles' group. It was love at first sight, and they married within months of meeting.

"Why wait?" Gene said when I asked about their first encounter. "I knew she was the gal for me."

Now in their late forties, Gene and Shirley obviously cared about one another. They approached this session as if nothing were seriously wrong, and I began with that point of view as well—though my opinion soon changed.

"So, tell me what has brought you here," I said.

"Well," Shirley began tentatively, smiling at Gene. "We have a wonderful relationship. But I think Gene may have a problem."

"Not as far as I'm concerned," Gene replied, smiling back at her. "I don't think it is anything we can't solve, but Shirley insisted we come here for a session or two. No offense, Doc, but I don't really give much credence to psychologists. I think we can solve our own problems. But I'll see a shrink if my sweetheart wants me to."

"I appreciate that, Gene. So, it must have taken something for you to agree to come in here."

"Not really. She's worth it."

Gene reached over and gave Shirley a pat on the knee.

I sat quietly, waiting for them to pursue the real issue for which they had sought counseling. Both appeared reluctant to share anything further. Finally, I broke the silence.

"So, what is this problem that needs our attention?"

"Gene likes to play blackjack at the casino," Shirley blurted. "I think it's a problem. He doesn't."

"Once a week or so I like to stop by the Lucky Eagle and play cards. I keep my spending in check."

"Is that really all of it?" Shirley asked.

"As far as I'm concerned, it is."

"You don't agree, Shirley?" I asked.

"Not exactly. It usually turns out to be the whole evening once he's down there, often two evenings a week. It eats up most of his paycheck, and we can't afford it."

Gene bristled. "When was the last time I spent my paycheck at the tables?"

"Remember three weeks ago when I called you on your cell, and you were still playing cards at eleven o'clock?"

Gene did his best to brush aside Shirley's criticism. "It doesn't happen often. I agreed to keep things in check, and I have."

Shirley looked at me and winced. "Does it sound like we have a problem?" she asked.

"I haven't heard enough to make that kind of determination," I said. "What is most important is whether you think there is a problem."

Having said that, I wondered if it was true. Is a couple always able to determine whether they have a problem? Or must someone outside the relationship sometimes render an opinion about what might be best? I know that when I feel sick, I am not the best person to determine what is ailing me.

"He doesn't think it's a problem," Shirley said, "and I'm not sure. He says gambling is just part of socializing with his friends. How do we know what's right?"

"I suggest that we look into this situation a little closer. Perhaps we'll be able to reach a conclusion about whether or not this is a problem that needs our attention."

I spent the rest of the session exploring both their relationship and "the problem" in more detail. What I discovered surprised me.

Gene was a full-fledged gambling addict and alcoholic. He not only liked to play blackjack, as he originally admitted, but enjoyed other games of chance as well. He was at the racetrack on many Saturdays. Reluctantly, he admitted that he had spent numerous paychecks on gambling and that it had played a role in the demise of his first marriage, though he emphasized the relationship had ended because his ex-wife had fallen in love with another man.

I was also surprised by Shirley's response. As the truth came out, she seemed intent on supporting her husband. She expressed only minimal concern for his gambling problems. She said she was proud of him for agreeing to attend the session. She commented that Gene had not wasted a paycheck on gambling in the past month or so. She went out of her way to avoid being overly critical of his behavior. She was clearly enabling his addiction.

I am alarmed when I see the kind of avoidance behavior Shirley displayed regarding Gene's gambling addiction. Others may see her excuses for Gene as models of love and support, but I find just the opposite to be true. Giving lip service to a life-damaging, marriage-threatening problem is equivalent to shrugging your shoulders when your diabetic son repeatedly refuses to take his insulin shot. We would never think of letting our children engage in this type of self-destructive behavior, yet we may be willing to look the other way when our spouses refuse to take responsibility for their catastrophic actions.

I can already hear the responses. "But, Doctor Hawkins, I can't change my mate's behavior. I have to let him work out his problems on his own."

I have addressed this type of enabling behavior at length in previous books, including *When Pleasing Others Is Hurting You.* I have clearly demonstrated the dramatic difference between trying to control another's addiction or destructive behavior and simply planting your head in the sand and ignoring it. Both are extreme behaviors with virtually no payoff.

Only one solution remains. You must speak the truth to your spouse and state clearly how you see the problem and the impact it is having on you and your family. Then you must lay out your expectations. You have no other option: You must hold your spouse accountable for his or her actions. Expecting anything less qualifies as codependency and, despite your wishes to the contrary, will only strengthen the problem. Ignoring things that need to be dealt with is never a solution. It only makes things worse.

As I uncovered the severity of Gene and Shirley's problems, I felt that I had only a short time with them—perhaps this one session—to make a difference because both were so caught up in denying the problem. Both saw it as a minor issue that they could easily resolve. Neither wanted to rock the boat. Both carefully avoided using the word *addiction* to describe Gene's gambling. Acknowledging it as such would almost certainly call for serious action—action they were not prepared to take.

As I shared my perception of the problem and its entrenched and debilitating nature, I could see Gene and Shirley emotionally leave the room. They did not want to hear what I had to say. Though Shirley had said she was interested in a professional opinion, she did not want to hear the truth. I suspected that Gene had heard many times before that his drinking and gambling could ruin his life unless he took action. But so far, he had not hit bottom. So far, his life had not collapsed enough for him to desire significant change.

As they left my office, they promised to consider what I had said—that they needed to make significant changes, or they would face serious consequences in the future. I told them as tactfully as possible that to skirt the real issues would do them no good. They needed major surgery if they wanted to root out the cancer in their marriage.

Incongruence

As I observed Gene and Shirley in my office that day, Gene's high level of denial did not surprise me as much as Shirley's apparent naïveté. What was she thinking? How could she know what she knew and fail to acknowledge how serious their problems were?

In addition to her naïveté and denial, the incongruence between her words and her emotions struck me. From her decision to come in for a professional opinion to her quick escape from my office, she exhibited a prickly inconsistency.

I remember conversations I'd had with a professional colleague who worked at an oncologist's office as a social worker. Some of her patients would arrive filled with fear and sobriety. They needed reassurance that the doctors would do everything possible for their loved one. Others seemed eerily detached from the process. They arrived smiling, as if they were coming in to order a new car and they had nothing to be concerned about. Whenever she saw this behavior, she knew she would have difficulty breaking through their denial so that they could honestly address the problem they were facing.

I surmised that Shirley felt ambivalent about her husband and his actions. After all, she had a lot on the line. Lest we become too critical of Shirley, we must remember that all of us struggle with an uncomfortable incongruence. Too often, we say we believe one thing but do something entirely different. We boldly ready ourselves to face a problem, only to back away in fear. Like Shirley, we announce that we are ready to stand up for what we believe, but then we retreat because the cost of change is too high. Molehills are far easier to scale than mountains.

Frog in the Kettle

As I watched Gene and Shirley head toward certain calamity, I thought of the old story of the frogs in the kettle.

A group of frogs was thrown into a kettle of boiling water. Using sound judgment, they immediately jumped out to safety. They did not need a focus group or board meeting to reach this decision. Their pain was sharp and instructive. *We better get out now if we want to live,* it told them.

Later, these same frogs were placed in a kettle of cold water. Soon, some began to notice a gradual increase in temperature.

First frog: "I think it's getting hot in here."

Second frog: "You're imagining things."

Third frog: "It's just the air temperature. We're fine."

First frog: "Well, I could swear it's getting hot, but maybe you're right."

As the story continues, the first frog elects to go along with the crowd. The frogs were oblivious to their peril and their eventual demise.

Studies actually seem to reinforce this fable. During my graduate studies in psychology, I learned of animals that remained in lethal situations when danger came on slowly.

As you consider Gene and Shirley's situation, or perhaps that of the frogs, you may feel you are immune. Think again. Ask yourself if your marriage faces problems that you hope will miraculously disappear.

Consider how these possible "frogs in the kettle" situations might apply to you or your mate:

- viewing pornography
- spending excessively
- exercising excessively as a way of fighting depression
- tiptoeing around your mate to avoid anger
- making excuses for your mate's alcohol use
- working excessively
- suspecting unfaithfulness but being afraid to talk about it
- bingeing and purging but denying the problem
- avoiding facing a diminishing sexual relationship

You will find "frogs in the kettle" anywhere you find denial, minimization, or avoidance of a problem. Failing to take full responsibility for our problems invariably leads to larger problems later.

Ask yourself, *What areas in my marriage do I tend to avoid? What problems do I need to face today?*

The Delight of Denial

Couples' avoidance of serious problems is clearly dangerous, so one wonders why denial is so rampant. People can rarely understand denial at the moment it occurs. Only in the rearview mirror can we see the power and damage denial causes. After all, when we're in denial we do not admit to the power of the problem. We are too blinded by the fog to see anything clearly.

I often listen to people reminisce about their lives, reflecting on how they were enamored with a particular situation or person and couldn't see the dark side until months later, when they were fully immersed in the problem. The woman who falls head over heals for the dashing man sometimes realizes she has projected many wonderful traits onto him because she wanted a white knight. Later, when reality sets in, she sees his grandiosity and self-centeredness and resents him for it. Reality finally crashes through the walls of denial.

Denial took its most potent bite out of my life more than 20 years ago when I was in graduate school working on my doctorate. I made the decision to return to school with the full cooperation of my family. But I could not see then, as I see now, the ravaging effects school and my workaholism would have on me and the people I loved.

When I finally decided to go back to school, I felt that I should continue to work so that my family could continue to enjoy a reasonable standard of living. However, I chose to work in my counseling office from dawn to dusk, six days a week. As the demands of school and work increased, I ignored the insidious negative effects on my health, marriage, and family. I made lots of excuses for working as hard as I did—all forms and fashions of denial.

I told myself and my family—quite forcefully—that my hard work was for them, not for me. I deluded myself into believing that my commitment to work was virtuous, and I prided myself on the long hours I was putting in.

I had no finish line. The harder I worked, the more I wanted to achieve. My behavior became addictive. I had completely subjugated myself—and, by extension, my family—to the power and influence of working more hours and making more money. All the while, I told myself that I was sacrificing for the sake of my wife and children. This was an incredible act of self-deception because I was really only trying to please and impress myself. Like Scrooge with his pile of gold coins, I counted the hours I worked and tabulated the money I made.

Friends and family members tried to caution me about working and studying so hard, but I refused to listen. I wanted to work long hours—I wanted to prove to myself and others that I could do it. I wanted to make as much money as possible and push my body to the limit. I was full of myself and full of denial.

I now look back on those years with severe regret. Although I accomplished a lot, I also missed out on many special moments in my sons' childhood years. I missed soccer matches, parent-teacher meetings, and evening tuck-ins. The toll on my family and me was enormous. My health declined, my marriage suffered, and my spiritual life became hollow.

I look back now with sadness and regret because I am keenly aware that my sons didn't care about money—they simply wanted more time with their father. They reacted to my extended absences by becoming clingy at some times and distant at others. My youngest son, Tyson, would lie awake until late in the evening, waiting for me to arrive home so that we could share a prayer. At the time, I was grateful for those precious moments, but now I see that my selfishness placed an unfair burden on him. He missed his father and sacrificed sleep in order to obtain a few minutes with me. If only I had been willing to give as much.

The distance between us often became difficult to handle. On the evenings I was home, my sons would sometimes treat me like an unexpected guest. At times, the conversations at the dinner table seemed stifled, as if I were interrupting the natural flow of the family. They had a rhythm, and it did not include me. When I was around, life was awkward for all of us. I can even recall times when my sons would say, "Dad, what are you doing home?" as if I didn't belong. I recoiled at the implication. "I want to spend time with my family," I would respond, simultaneously wounded and annoyed.

Had things really regressed to the point where my own sons were unsure of their father's role in the family?

My oldest son, Josh, replaced me with outside activities. At the time, I told myself that his interest in sports and other hobbies was healthy. Now I see how much he needed a healthy relationship with his father. Instead of taking batting practice with me, he spent his time at the ballpark taking his practice from someone else's dad. Instead of throwing the football with me in the backyard, he got his companionship from the video games in our basement.

The impact on my marriage was immeasurable. I tried to assuage my wife's anger by insisting that my absences did not need to have a negative effect on our relationship. This was, of course, a ludicrous argument. How could our marriage be normal or healthy when I wasn't even there to participate in it?

I made agreement after agreement with her, promising to reduce my workweek. I was like an alcoholic, who tries to make deals about drinking. She would attempt to bargain with me, though her words seldom had any impact. Promises made simply became promises broken. The inevitable effect was a loosening of the bonds that had held us together. Laughter was no longer a part of our lives. Instead, an insidious tension always seemed to be lurking in the shadows.

God got less from me, as well. Since I was absent from myself, I could hardly be fully present to my wife, my children, or my God. I still loved the Lord, but I gave Him only the leftovers of my life. As I had done with my wife, I also made promises with God. And, of course, I broke those without a second thought. I shortened my prayer times, limited my Bible studies, and gave fellowship with others a backseat to the other god—work. All the while, I became more depleted inside.

Unfortunately, my workaholism did not abate, even as I began to realize its impact. Engrossed in my denial, I ignored my family's confrontations. Only when my body began screaming for relief, years later, did I come to a greater understanding of the effects of workaholism. Only then did I admit that I could not continue to work at the pace I had been maintaining for so many years.

I didn't surrender to natural limitations without a fight. I struggled like a boxer fighting well past his prime. For the longest time, I felt my body was betraying me. How could I still want to work so hard and yet be unable to do so because of physical limitations? My stamina was gone, and my need for sleep and rest increased—normal events that I had previously ignored. Still I railed against others who were able to work long hours without apparent negative side effects. It wasn't fair.

In many ways, I was like a deep-sea diver, so caught up in the dive that I discounted my disorientation and "forgot" to heed the call to return to the surface for oxygen. Such divers are hyper-focused but on the wrong things. They miscalculate their remaining time. In essence, they fail to be rigorously honest with themselves. When we are busy whistling Dixie and avoiding our problems, we are not addressing the task at hand, and the results may be disastrous.

Fortunately, I eventually heeded the siren. I was forced to change my lifestyle to save my family relationships—but not without the residue of years of neglect.

Usually, defeat has slapped us across the face many times before we finally get it: *This path is going to cause great pain if you don't change your behavior.* If we keep whistling Dixie, as if these mountains were just molehills, we will ultimately face staggering consequences.

The Dance of Deception

Although we may readily agree that honesty is the best policy, we still resist it. We continue to shrink back from talking to our mate in an honest and straightforward manner. Ever since the fiasco in the Garden, we have been hiding.

God attempted to have an honest encounter with Adam and Eve, but they were so busy pointing fingers, they never came clean about the matter of sin. I think people will always struggle with telling the truth. I think we are destined to use huge quantities of energy to present ourselves in the most favorable light. We seem to have an ingrained nature to see others as the culprits and ourselves as the victims. With this posturing, truth doesn't stand a chance.

As I conduct countless hours of marriage counseling, I see individuals dodge and weave in their dance of deception. They often don't want to change. Rather, they expect other people to change to meet their needs. They don't want to focus on their part in the problem—they want to focus on how other people have victimized them. Wanting the easy way out, they give as little ground as possible, gaining as much ground as they can for themselves.

Take a moment to consider your own marriage. How much are you really willing to share with your spouse? How truthful are you about the problems in your relationship? How easily do you take responsibility for wrongdoing? How easily do you ask for forgiveness? I suspect you will agree with me that candor in marriage is a rare commodity.

Sam Keen, in his book *To Love and Be Loved,* makes this claim:

> Love is the original and only enduring free speech movement. It unlocks the tongue, allows us to talk about anything, creates wholesome speech. The truth, the whole truth, and nothing but the truth is never told in court. It can only be spoken within a sanctuary created by those who care for each other unconditionally.[1]

Only those who care for each other unconditionally can speak the truth to each other. We speak the truth when we have the power of God working in our lives.

"But if we walk in the light, as he is in the light, we have fellowship with one another, and the blood of Jesus, his Son, purifies us from all sin" (1 John 1:7).

The Power of Codependency

Shirley did not really want to know the truth about Gene's problem. After all, she had lost out on love before and feared she might lose out again. Her wounds were finally starting to heal, now that she had found someone who cared for her and vowed he would never leave her. But Gene's caring and devotion came with a price.

Because of her desire to have it all—to be in love and live happily ever after with her knight in shining armor—she refused to see the dents in his armor. She refused to see what was obvious to most outside observers.

In spite of all her positive characteristics, Shirley's relationship with Gene was dominated by her *codependency*. Codependency is *any attempt to ignore, and thereby reinforce, another's weaknesses*. Her world of codependency meant that she chose to not fully see the truth of Gene's addiction to gambling and alcohol.

Allowing codependency in marriage is a critical mistake. It is a problem that creates molehills out of mountains. It ignores a cancer instead of seeking a cure. It leaves husband and wife unable to find intimacy because they are not truly honest with one another.

A classic example of a card-carrying codependent was Edith Bunker from the long-running TV series *All in the Family*. Although we may have laughed at Archie's many foibles, his bombastic style, and his flagrant prejudices, they were really quite tragic. All the while, Edith seemed oblivious to the damage his attitudes and behaviors were having on their marriage and Archie's other relationships.

Instead of confronting Archie about his obnoxious and self-aggrandizing behavior, Edith ignored it. She danced around his anger, attempting to stay out of the fray as much as possible. Her character was so self-effacing, we wonder if anyone out there is really like her. I assure you, to one degree or another, many of us dance around problems as Edith did to avoid the heat of honesty.

In her wonderful book *Coupleship,* Sharon Wegscheider-Cruse tells us how to overcome codependency in marriage. She believes that many problems can be corrected in marriage if a couple will agree to live out the following values:

- *Honesty of feelings*—couples express feelings of passion as well as vulnerability. They give each other permission to voice anger, disappointment, and jealousy. In addition, each person is willing to share feelings of hurt, guilt, inadequacy, and fear.

- *Courage*—Both people contribute to the partnership even if doing so is difficult. They expect no more from the partnership than they are ready to give.

- *Spontaneity*—even though each partner respects and values the other's responsibilities and commitments, each is willing to put a bookmark in self-activity to respond to the want or need of the other.

- *Responsibility*—as we become more aware of the impact we have on those around us, we are able to respond in loving ways. Once we learn to say, "I don't understand," "I am sorry," "Will you tell me again?" or "It was my fault"—all of these admissions and responses get easier. We learn that our goals are closeness, support, and intimacy, rather than victory, power, and control.

- *Diversity*—when we get to know another person wholly, we discover ideas, thoughts, and values that are a bit different (or perhaps a lot different) from our own. We can appreciate human diversity instead of having to defeat it or feel inadequate.[2]

Codependency has been called "the urge to merge." We so want to fit in, to not disappoint another person. We dare not risk someone getting angry with us or disdaining our opinion. But this desire to avoid ruffling any feathers ultimately sabotages a marriage. It becomes a barrier to honest, healthy interaction—in any relationship.

Harriet Lerner, in her book *The Dance of Anger,* shares another reason people fear honesty. She believes that one of our greatest fears is the fear of separateness.

> Separation anxiety may creep up on us whenever we shift to a more autonomous, nonblaming position in a relationship, or even when we simply consider the possibility. Sometimes such anxiety is based on a realistic fear that if we assume a bottom-line stance ("I am sorry, but I will not do what you are asking of me"), we risk losing a relationship or a job. More often, and more crucially, separation anxiety is based on an underlying discomfort with separateness and individuality that has its roots in our early family experience, where the unspoken expectation may have been that we keep a lid on our expressions of self. Daughters are especially sensitive to such demands and may become far more skilled at protecting the relational "we" than asserting the autonomous "I".[3]

Who cannot relate to this preoccupation with protecting the relational *we?* Who among us is not concerned with keeping a relationship at least stable, if not warm and fuzzy? Although we must be concerned with keeping our relationships healthy, we cannot achieve that health if we sacrifice honesty and healthy contact.

Not Peace but Division

Christ taught much about being at peace with others. But He also taught about division. He chastens us to see things for the way they are and take appropriate action.

> I have come to bring fire on earth, and how I wish it were already kindled!...Do you think I came to bring peace on earth? No, I tell you, but division. From now on there will be five in one family divided...father against son and son against father, mother against daughter and daughter against mother, mother-in-law against daughter-in-law and daughter-in-law against mother-in-law (Luke 12:49-53).

Wow! Those words have got to rattle our codependent cages! His message challenges us regarding honesty and differences. Sometimes we must say it the way it is, and mincing words will not do. We must occasionally look our mates in the eye and say we are unhappy with the way things are. We do not approve of their excessive drinking, spending, work, drug use, deception, and yes, even avoidance of conflict. We cannot sit with the silence any longer. Let the chips fall where they may—it is time to talk!

Christ repeatedly addresses the tension between truth and deception, light and darkness. We are often tempted to minimize problems, to hide the actions we know to be shameful. But we also know intuitively that to do so, to hide our dark deeds, is to bring about more shame and distance from our spouse. Listen again to the words of Christ:

> Light has come into the world, but men loved darkness instead of light because their deeds were evil. Everyone who does evil hates the light, and will not come into the

light for fear that his deeds will be exposed. But whoever lives by the truth comes into the light, so that it may be seen plainly that what he has done has been through God (John 3:19-21).

The Cost of Honesty

And so we begin to understand the importance of speaking the truth in love. But as we consider doing this, we also must contemplate the risk of honesty. Being honest can be terrifying, especially for those who have mates who do not want to hear the truth.

So what is the cost?

First, *the cost of honesty includes the rigor of examining ourselves and knowing what we really think.* This may sound like a simple task, but it is not. Many of us are so used to fitting in—molding our opinions to those around us—that we do not know exactly what we believe or why we believe it.

Some time ago, I began a practice I now recommend to all my clients. I began spending a few minutes every day journaling to reflect on my life and understand the events that affect me. The recipe I recommend is to write what you feel, think, and want. I have found that a steady diet of this kind of journaling will lead to a keener sense of what is important to me.

Why have I, and so many others, found this exercise to be valuable and potent? Because it honors and amplifies a relationship with yourself. If you don't know what you think, what you feel, or what you want, you are like a ship without a rudder, drifting with the tides. I am not recommending that we worship the self, but I do believe that without this primary relationship, all others will falter. Even our relationship with God is predicated on first knowing who we are.

Journaling is also a wonderful spiritual exercise. I often read a portion of Scripture and then chew on it for a few moments. As I meditate on these morsels, I write what I believe the Lord may be saying to me. Doing this on a regular basis gives me a springboard from which I can move forward in my life.

Second, *the cost of honesty includes taking the time and energy to see your mate as distinct from yourself.* True love means seeing your spouse as an individual and relating to him or her as such.

Consider this exercise:

Next time you sit down with your spouse, do your best to *really* listen. Not just to the words, but to the silent spaces. Honest relating takes incredible energy. Barbara Sher, in her book *It's Only Too Late If You Don't Start Now,* describes this challenge:

> To see someone else clearly, not to look into the mirror of your own desire or to dress up the beloved with the scrim of your favorite fantasy, or to reinvent him for your own uses...Loving what is actually in front of you can come only when you've outgrown illusions of perfection— yours or anyone else's—and when you keep the freedom to build your life at the same time as respecting the other's right to do the same.[4]

Third, *the cost of honesty, of truly expressing how we feel, is that we may be criticized.* If we put ourselves "out there," we leave ourselves open to ridicule.

Being criticized is never fun. Hearing someone say, "I don't care what you think," is frightening. Generally, I view this bravado as dishonest and unhealthy. We need to be able to be hurt. We need to have thin enough skin so that others can make true contact with us.

Fourth, *the cost of honesty is that conflict may result.* When we dare to be honest, when we dare to address a difficult issue, we may move out of our circle of comfort and into the arena of anxiety. Harriet Goldhor Lerner, in her book *The Dance of Intimacy,* reflects on this:

We all have emotionally charged issues in our family that are difficult to address. We may all find ourselves confronting a choice between authenticity and harmony in a particular relationship. We all have to deal with powerful countermoves and "Change back!" reactions—both from within and without—if we define the "I" apart from the roles and rules of family and culture.[5]

When we dare to spill the beans about relational secrets, we will most certainly stir up tension at first. The cost is high, but the rewards are great as well.

Finally, *the cost of honesty includes being free.* How is that a cost, you might ask? Let's reflect back on Gene and Shirley. They have been living in bondage for a long time. How would Gene and Shirley feel if they were free?

Actually, Gene and Shirley did decide to face their problem. It was not easy, but they gradually agreed to look deeper into the gambling issue that brought them to counseling and consider what his addiction and her avoidance were costing their marriage. Progress was not a direct, linear movement, but they continued to return for counseling and eventually decided that Gene needed to get additional treatment for his problem. We contacted the local Gambler's Anonymous group, and that, combined with his men's group at church, provided the help he needed to deal honestly with his problem.

And what about Shirley? She had to come face-to-face with her reluctance to deal honestly with Gene's addiction. She had to accept that it was no molehill but rather a mountain that they needed to climb. Her part was to come out of denial and accept her own codependency. She found a support group for spouses of gambling addicts. At first, the result was an uncomfortable freedom. But now, months later, both Shirley and Gene are rejoicing in their new freedom.

One Step at a Time

Change is almost always frightening. That is why a crisis is often necessary for us to break free from the status quo. A calamity can become a messenger of positive changes.

Change never happens in one fell swoop. Gene and Shirley's move toward freedom included fits and starts, and I suspect the same will be true for you. Don't expect that you will make a decision to change and that will be that. If only change were that simple.

Expect that change will be difficult. Expect that looking candidly into the face of any problem will be challenging. To stop whistling Dixie is not easy if that has been a pattern in your marriage. Expect to pay a price for change, but the growth will be worth the cost.

The first step is seeing the mountain you need to climb. Deciding to embark on the journey of change is the most important step. After that, everything else can fall into place. You can climb the mountain one step at a time—together with your mate and God. After all, if God is for us, who can be against us?

Chapter Four

Stop Speaking Greek:
The Importance of Communicating Clearly

When words are many, sin is not absent,
but he who holds his tongue is wise.
The tongue of the righteous is choice silver.
—PROVERBS 10:19-20

The counseling session in my office was like a scene from the old Abbott and Costello comedy routine "Who's on First?"—except this was no comedy.

I had been working with Kevin and Kendra for several weeks. They were a couple in their forties, married 16 years with two preteen children. They told me their marriage had been stable and relatively happy with a few bumps along the way. Recently, however, they felt an inability to clearly communicate with one another, especially when emotions ran high.

We had been working together to improve their communication skills. Things were going well until they had a heated encounter in one of their counseling sessions.

"I don't like the way he spends money," Kendra said abruptly.

Kevin rolled his eyes in exasperation.

"What's the problem?" I asked.

"I just don't like it, and he knows it," she said again, even more forcefully.

"I hear your frustration," I said, "but can you be specific about what bothers you about his spending?" She kept talking as if she hadn't heard me.

"He knows what I don't like about it, but he still keeps doing it. He didn't use to be so bad about it, but it's gotten worse lately. Sometimes, I think he's mean. He spends money we don't have, and I have to do the worrying about it."

"Never mind, Doc," Kevin said. "I know what she's getting at. She resents my motorcycle. It's easier for her to focus on me than look at herself. That's it."

"Is it the motorcycle, Kendra?" I asked her.

"No, I can understand a man needing a motorcycle. I guess all men have to have a garage full of big-boy toys," she said sarcastically. "But he blows money lots of other ways and it drives me nuts."

"Like what?" Kevin said angrily. "I work my tail off so I can have some nice things, and you resent them. I told you when we got married that I work to play, and that's not going to change. I make sure I spend time at home with you and the kids."

"That's not the point," Kendra said firmly. "And besides, you're gone a lot of weekends riding with the guys." She paused for a moment.

"I just don't like the way you spend money, plain and simple. I don't know how else to say it." Kendra continued to look at me, giving Kevin the cold shoulder.

At that point Kevin leaned forward in his chair, more irritated than ever.

"But you spend money, too! You have a closet full of clothes, and I would like to say a few things about that. How many shoes do you really need? You and your mother have spending issues of your own, if you ask me."

"It's not the same."

Kendra turned away and looked out the window. Kevin looked at me, as if asking for help.

There we were, right back where we had started. We had passed "Go" but had not collected two hundred dollars. Instead, we were well on our way to matrimonial jail, which is filled with hurt feelings, resentment, bitterness, and—worst of all—*no progress!*

This was the point in the session when I thought of the classic comedic team, Abbott and Costello. Who really was on first? I certainly didn't know exactly what Kevin and Kendra's problem was or what they wanted from each other.

And if I was confused, sitting on the outside looking in, I can only imagine how they must have felt on the inside of this mess. Sorting out their problem was like trying to take one paper clip from a box, only to find that all of the clips are tangled together.

Why are Kendra and Kevin having such a tough time? Why can't they get to the heart of the matter, deal with the issues at hand, resolve them, and get on to bigger and better things?

Because their conversation is obscure, vague, indirect, passive-aggressive, and simply nonproductive.

They suffer from our fourth critical mistake: speaking Greek instead of clearly and concisely saying what we need and want.

We laugh at Abbott and Costello's plight. They talk in code, each failing to define their terms or slow down the conversation enough to really know what the other means.

Because we are standing on the outside of their encounter, we can laugh. Perhaps we snicker at Kevin and Kendra as well. But anyone who has been on the inside of such a conversation knows this is anything but funny.

Defensiveness

Is one person right and the other person wrong? Do we align ourselves with Kendra, who seems to have a case against Kevin regarding his expensive toys but is unwilling to fully articulate her feelings? Do we side with Kevin, who works hard for his toys and seems genuine about asking Kendra what she wants? Perhaps neither deserves our allegiance because neither is communicating in a way that will solve the problem. Both seem to be speaking Greek, which is only adding to their problems.

Anyone who has been in an intimate relationship knows that when both parties speak Greek, the outcome is usually miscommunication. Frustration, anger, and defensiveness soon follow.

Frustration and anger are emotions, but defensiveness is an attitude that stops communication, a mind-set that says, *I want to be understood, but you're not understanding me. On the other hand, I don't really want to listen to what you have to say.*

This mind-set is immature and intolerant, but it should not surprise us. Everyone wants to be heard and understood. No one wants to be maligned. The more fragile we feel, the more brittle we are, and the more we rely on excessive defensiveness.

Susan Heitler and Abigail Hirsch, in their workbook *The Power of Two,* are very concerned about defensiveness. "The downside to defensive walls is that while they may prevent hurtful comments from entering, they also block out potentially useful new information. Listening to learn will generally be more effective than defensive responses."[1]

Let's consider the impact of defensiveness in marriage. First, *defensiveness stops communication.* As a general rule, when you or your partner becomes defensive, effective communications stops. The noise you are making may sound like communication, but it is no longer healthy and clear. It is now a clash over whose opinion will win out. Perceptions narrow and battle lines emerge. You are now engaged in a debate, not a discussion.

Second, *defensiveness stops us from seeing each other's viewpoint.* Screens go up, our vision gets foggy, and communication becomes muddled. We see only our point of view and defend it vigorously. We stop working at seeing or understanding our mate's point of view. If we recognize it at all, we immediately search for ways to find fault with it.

Third, *we don't express our position clearly.* When we are feeling defensive, we tend to over-defend our viewpoint. We take on rigid opinions and don't state our positions accurately. We are no longer flexible and open to new possibilities. Again, effective communication has stopped.

Fourth, *defensiveness keeps us from dealing with sensitive topics.* Some topics—such as drinking, excessive spending, eating disorders, and sexual difficulties—are virtually forbidden under the best of circumstances. When we approach them, defensiveness heightens. The message is clear: Avoid sensitive topics until things calm down.

Finally, *defensiveness compounds unhealthy communication.* Excessive defensiveness give rise to competition, argumentativeness, hostility, denial, and blaming. Defensiveness brings out the worst in people and has no place in a growing, vibrant marriage.

Crazy-Making

We watch Kevin and Kendra's style of communicating in frustration. We've been there ourselves, communicating so awkwardly we wonder if we or our spouses are to blame. Are we speaking unclearly, or are they simply trying to sabotage any effort at honest communication?

We may also struggle to accurately interpret what our spouses are saying, only to end up in a downward spiral, hovering dangerously near "the plunger," which triggers the emotional explosion we are trying so desperately to avoid.

In some conversations like this, people are simply not listening carefully. But other conversations reflect a more serious problem. If your communication sounds like Kendra and Kevin's on a regular basis, your relationship may be afflicted with *crazy-making*. If so, it needs immediate attention.

People are crazy-making when they say one thing on the surface but really mean something else. You may sense that your partner is asking for something but will not or cannot come right out and say what it is. Because the message never comes through plainly, you cannot deal with it in an honest and straightforward manner. If you receive messages that say one thing but mean something else, you will likely become frustrated, angry, and confused. You will feel as if you are going crazy.

The term *crazy-making* obviously has a powerful, negative slant. It implies that one partner is a "crazy-maker"—someone who is intent on making his or her partner crazy or at least furious. However, I don't believe that most crazy-making behavior is essentially malicious. So why would someone resort to such indirect, manipulative communication? Several reasons come to mind.

First, *asking for exactly what we want can be frightening*. For many of us, hiding behind a veil of indirect communication is much easier. We hope our spouses will read our minds and automatically meet our needs, but as you might expect, this rarely happens.

Second, *we risk rejection*. In response to our request, our spouses might look at us and say, "Are you nuts? I'm not going to do that." Then we are faced with an even larger problem: Now what are we going to do?

Third, *we may be too meek and passive*. This might be a style we have employed throughout our lives and now use in our marriage. It is an indication that we have not learned the art of direct, clear communication.

Finally, *speaking in a clear and straightforward manner takes great effort*. Lucid, honest communication is anything but easy. Communication is a refined skill, and it takes work to master.

What can you do if you are dealing with a partner who uses crazy-making as a tactic to avoid honest communication? Bach and Deutsch offer these suggestions in their book, *Stop! You're Driving Me Crazy.*[2]

- Step back from the situation and evaluate what is happening. Consider why you might be feeling confused or manipulated.

- Consider what might underlie the crazy-making, such as your spouse feeling rejected, powerless, or fearful about asking for change.

- Don't react hostilely to the crazy-making, even if you are tempted to do so. Ask for clarification, don't attack. The problem is not the person but rather his or her inability to ask clearly for what he or she needs. Try to bring the desired changes into the open.

- Respect your spouse's right to honest information, as well as his or her feelings, space, and power. Try to lessen your partner's fear of asking for what he or she needs.

- Don't read minds or make assumptions. Share your feelings and make yourself vulnerable. Keep the discussion focused on the issue at hand.

- Check out your hunches. See if what you think is happening is truly happening. Try to determine what your spouse is really asking for.

- Arrive at a fair compromise that involves both of you making desired changes.

I have found another skill to be immensely helpful for myself and for those I counsel. It is simply this: *Speak from your most vulnerable self.* Let me illustrate.

Recently, I became embroiled in one of those obscure, Greek-speaking conversations with a dear friend. As is often the case, it began innocently enough and escalated quickly.

I was out for an evening walk with Christie, and I mentioned that I was considering working late one day a week. I planned to take an extended break in the morning so I wouldn't increase my total work hours. I wanted her encouragement for this plan even though I had previously asked her to hold me accountable for working too many hours at my office. She was immediately concerned.

"I thought you weren't going to work any evenings," she said.

I bristled. My work hours have always been and still are a touchy subject for me. I wanted encouragement from her, not criticism.

"No," I said abruptly, "I said I was not going to work any *additional* hours in a day."

"But even if you take a break during the day, you'll still be at the office longer than usual."

I clammed up, fighting my urge to bark at her. How dare she hold me accountable, even if I had given her permission to do so? We walked along in silence as I considered how I wanted to respond. As I tried to fight my defensiveness, I decided to speak from my most vulnerable self.

"Christie, I've asked you to hold me accountable, and now I feel anxious about doing so. I feel criticized *and* convicted. I want to take a minute and think about what you said instead of defending myself, which won't help either of us."

"I'm just giving you my opinion," she said cautiously. "You asked me to tell you what I thought about this issue."

"Yes, I did. I still want your feedback, and this reaction has to do with me, not you. Give me a couple of minutes to process my reaction."

Some of you may be thinking this conversation belongs on the Mister Rogers' show and has no place in real life. Or perhaps it seems like something out of some psychology textbook and has no application for your marriage. Wrong!

Acting thoughtfully and cautiously was extremely difficult for me, but our friendship is worth the effort. You too can learn to monitor your defensiveness, own your feelings, and share them at appropriate times.

Dishonesty and Pretending

Another way to speak Greek in a marriage is to be dishonest. Being straightforward and truthful in a relationship is difficult. Acting like a chameleon, always transforming ourselves into whatever the other person expects us to be, is far easier. But this is simply another form of codependence.

In the scenario above, I was sending Christie a mixed message. In essence, I was saying, "Please risk telling me when you think I am slipping into old, destructive behavior. But whatever you do, don't upset me."

Wow! How dishonest of me. How manipulative. By telling Christie that I wanted feedback, I opened the door to sounding self-righteous. But when the rubber hit the road, I was unwilling to stand behind my request. I was being dishonest even though I hadn't intended to.

As we look critically at Kendra, we see that she too refused to be honest. She refused to put herself out there and state directly what she expected of Kevin. Instead, she seemed to believe he was obligated to read her mind.

John Bradshaw, in his groundbreaking book *Bradshaw On: The Family,* explains why we speak in disguised, obscure ways:

> We are taught to be nice and polite. We are taught that these behaviors (most often lies) are better than telling the truth. We are taught above all to pretend we are not feeling the things we are feeling. Our churches, schools and politics are rampant with teaching dishonesty (saying

things we don't mean and pretending to feel ways we don't feel). We smile when we feel sad; laugh nervously when dealing with grief; laugh at jokes we don't think are funny; tell people things to be polite that we surely don't mean, like we have to get together some time.[3]

Surely Bradshaw is being overly harsh. You are an honest person and say what you mean. Right?

I don't relish making this public confession, but I know that I do not. Bradshaw's words bite, and they fit me more than I would like to admit. If I were truly being honest, if I were speaking straight, I would have said this to Christie:

"Christie, I want to be free from the exhaustion I feel from working too hard. But I don't really want to change. So when I ask you to confront me when you see irresponsible behavior emerging, I am not being honest. I don't want to be confronted. I really only want to be encouraged. I want praise for the changes I am making, and I want you to wink when you see something that smacks of irresponsibility on my part."

Okay. There's the truth. I am not sure how it would fly in a conversation with Christie, but at least it would be honest. At least it would be a starting point for sincere conversation.

Don Miguel Ruiz wrote a bestselling book titled *The Four Agreements*. When it came out, folks everywhere were asking, "Have you read *The Four Agreements*? You've got to read it." At first, I was surprised by the book's success. Frankly, it didn't seem all that profound. But something about it grabbed me. Ruiz's most essential standard was to *be impeccable with your word*. This is not as easy as it sounds. He suggests that this is a transforming principle. Tell the truth—the precise truth for who you are today. Say what you mean and mean what you say. When we fail to do that, we are not only being dishonest with others but with ourselves as well—and this is terribly destructive to our self-esteem and the well-being of our relationships.

On the importance of being impeccable with our word, Ruiz says, "Through the word you express your creative power. It is through the word that you manifest everything...What you dream, what you feel, and what you really are, will all be manifested through the word."[4]

Reluctant Truth Tellers

Ruiz's words are hardly new. The Scriptures frequently encourage us to tell the truth. Both the Old and New Testaments tell us to speak clearly and directly that which God has laid on our hearts.

I am reminded of the Lord's encounter with Moses, a man who would become a great leader. Yet in spite of his giftedness, he apparently wasn't impressed with his skills and argued that he was not qualified to be the Lord's mouthpiece.

You may recall that God directed Moses to rally the Israelites and to perform miracles demonstrating God's power and abiding presence with him. God called Moses to lead Israel out of their bondage in Egypt. But even after God had shown His power, Moses faltered.

"O Lord, I have never been eloquent, neither in the past, nor since you have spoken to your servant. I am slow of speech and tongue."

The LORD said to him, "Who gave man his mouth? Who makes him deaf or mute? Who gives him sight or makes him blind? Is it not I, the LORD? Now go; I will help you speak and will teach you what to say."

But Moses said, "O Lord, please send someone else to do it."

Then the LORD's anger burned against Moses and he

said, "What about your brother, Aaron the Levite? I know
he can speak well" (Exodus 4:10-14).

After receiving such gifts of leadership and witnessing so many
demonstrations of God's power—not to mention the timely opportunity of rescuing his people from slavery—Moses was still hesitant
to speak. We can understand why the Lord was frustrated with him.
But who among us doesn't also understand the trepidation of speaking truth to masses of people? What if they will not listen, as was
Moses' fear? What if they mock us, which also happened to Moses?
Even though we have seen God's power in our lives and have been
given the Holy Spirit—the "Spirit of truth"—we still recoil from
speaking out when the opportunity presents itself.

Jesus experienced His frustration with His reluctant disciples.
One of the most poignant examples occurs with Peter before the cru-
cifixion. Jesus had, of course, prophesied this event in the courtyard.
A servant girl of the high priest asks Peter if he had been with Jesus.
Here was an incredible opportunity to tell the truth and be a witness
for his Lord. Instead, Peter speaks Greek.

"I don't know or understand what you're talking about," Peter says.

But the girl does not give up. She knows what she knows. She says
to those gathered around, "This fellow is one of them." Again, he
denies it.

Now others join in the discussion. "Surely you are one of them,
for you are a Galilean."

You might think Peter would finally talk straight. The jig is up. But
instead, he ups the ante. "He began to call down curses on himself,
and he swore to them. 'I don't know this man you're talking about'"
(Mark 14:66-72).

At this the rooster crowed, and Peter recalled the words Jesus had
spoken to him—and he wept.

And we weep as well as we discover some of Moses and Peter in us. We look back on critical times in our lives when we could have said something truthful, something powerful. There we were, in our own dark, cold, scary place, with someone staring at us, waiting for us to be direct and truthful. And we shriveled—or danced.

We are reluctant to tell the truth, to say it the way it is. We hold back because of our fear, shame, or intimidation. We beat around the bush or tell outright lies to avoid these threats. Or, like Peter, we try to use confabulation—by speaking Greek—to distract those pressing us for the straight truth.

Withholding Truth

As we consider this notion of being truthful, you might think of times when withholding the truth is best. Perhaps speaking Greek or dancing around the issues is sometimes the best thing to do. After all, our partners might be vulnerable and might not take critical feedback well. Tiptoeing around them in these cases might be all right. We may tell ourselves that we are withholding information so we won't hurt someone, but this is rarely the case. Rather, we usually protect ourselves from vulnerability, playing it safe, using our dishonesty as a rationale for withholding the truth. Furthermore, even if we were trying to "protect" someone, this is a dubious exercise. Since when do others need our protection?

I am not advocating that we march into the lives of those we care about and pontificate our version of the truth. Holding ourselves up as the last bastion of truth and then righteously sharing our position with our partners is a sure recipe for disaster. No one wants to be confronted in this way. Yet prickly confrontation does have its place in marriage.

Scott Peck, in his book *The Road Less Traveled,* says, "The final and possibly the greatest risk of love is the risk of exercising power with humility. The most common example of this is the act of loving confrontation."

But Peck does not advocate waltzing into another's life and sharing wisdom from a superior position. This is not biblical, helpful, or prudent. Rather, Peck asserts that we must offer criticism "with a belief that one is probably right arrived at through scrupulous self-doubting and self-examination." Arrogance is always destructive and unproductive. Words laced with humility are helpful and often successful in instructing another.

Humble words are typically more helpful than commands. Paul's writings are suffused with injunctions to "bear with the failings of the weak" (Romans 15:1). "May the God who gives endurance and encouragement give you a spirit of unity among yourselves as you follow Christ Jesus, so that with one heart and mouth you may glorify the God and Father of our Lord Jesus Christ. Accept one another, then, just as Christ accepted you" (Romans 15:5-7).

However, Peck also goes on to tell us about the damage that comes from dancing around the truth with our mate.

> To fail to confront when confrontation is required for the nurture of spiritual growth represents a failure to love equally as much as does thoughtless criticism or condemnation and other forms of active deprivation of caring… Mutual loving confrontation is a significant part of all successful and meaningful human relationships. Without it the relationship is either unsuccessful or shallow.[5]

Judgments and Prejudices

Dedication to the truth—the avoidance of speaking Greek—and a willingness to be honest in our marriages demand a great deal from us. They require us to be honest, to be humble, and to lay aside our assumptions and judgments about others. They also require an open mind and a life of self-examination so that we are aware of our weaknesses and prejudices.

The Pharisees were judgmental people, and Jesus called them hypocrites on many occasions. They were routinely arrogant, posturing their self-righteousness in front of others, though their hearts were not so clean. To be called "pharisaical" is now synonymous with living a duplicitous life. It is the epitome of speaking Greek.

Even the disciples were judgmental. Rather than speaking of love, they were often unduly critical of each other. You will recall that one of their judgmental tirades was against the weakest of the weak—children (Matthew 19). Essentially they said, "These little children are bugging us. They can't teach us anything. Get them out of here."

But Christ offered a fresh perspective. We are to be innocent like children, accepting like children, open like children, tender like children.

We quickly criticize the disciples for their reactions, but we must ask ourselves whether they are different from our own. Do we sometimes place ourselves above or apart from others? How does that create a barrier to intimacy? How does it stop us from really listening?

Although it is a scary proposition, I encourage you to set aside your entrenched beliefs so that you can really listen to your mate—and others.

- Are you open to new ideas and positions?
- Are you willing to hold yourself to the same standard you hold others to?
- Are you willing to be accountable to others for your beliefs and behavior?

Attention

People have said that the highest form of love we can give to others is to truly attend to them. In its simplest form, attending means really listening. And if we truly listen, we will probably rid ourselves of much of our Greek-speaking since that kind of gibberish comes from wanting to hear what *we* have to say rather than really listening to what *our mate* is saying.

Recently, I had the opportunity to practice this kind of attending. At a workshop on domestic violence, I heard a youth describe how he had violently killed his parents. Though I knew in advance that the violence was an act of retribution for years of violence and neglect propagated upon him and his brothers, revenge of this kind seemed incredibly heinous. But I wanted to hear what this young man had to say, and I knew that if I listened through the ears of one judging him I would not learn anything.

The hour that followed brought me to tears. This rugged teenager, dressed in sweatshirt, ball cap, and jeans, told of years of abuse by his parents. I heard of the atrocities perpetrated on him and his brothers and how he had taken it upon himself to save his siblings by killing his mother and father. I heard of the tortuous preparation for the killings and the horrific guilt he has since endured. I listened as he told about the months of incarceration that followed his admission of guilt.

This was not an easy listen for me. Although I was not personally involved, I still had to practice what Scott Peck calls "bracketing." It requires temporarily giving up one's self, prejudices, and beliefs, and attending to new information. It is, as Peck says, an opportunity to "silence the familiar and welcome the strange."[6] It is a time to set aside present needs, past experiences, and future expectations so that you can attend to the present.

And how does this apply to marriage? Actually, it needs to take place every day. We must practice bracketing so that we can see our mates for who they are, not who we want them to be. We can speak frankly, and even be critical, while holding out the possibility that things are not as they seem. We must practice giving our mates the benefit of the doubt. Could it be that they are really not trying to hurt us? Could it be that they really want to save their marriages as much as we do? Could it be...?

From this "empty" space we are able to do what I call *soulful listening*. This is where we listen not only to what is being said but also to what is not being said. We listen to our mates' themes, to the hurts and desires they bring to us each day. When we attend to their deepest longings, we listen them into being. We are midwives to their souls. We have set our own needs aside, and so we are able to more effectively champion our partners.

Taking Responsibility

Recently I offered a Transitions Support Group to my church and community. I had no idea who might come or what needs they might bring. When the doors opened, people of all ages flooded in.

A 40-year-old woman had just come through an unwanted divorce and desperately needed support. A 50-year-old woman had moved from across the country to our small town and needed a sense of community. A 25-year-old man, recently separated, was filled with jagged individualism and irritation and a deep need for a helping hand. An older woman had been through numerous violent relationships and couldn't seem to escape the pattern.

Different voices. Different needs. How could I bring cohesion to the group? I reminded myself repeatedly that I was a facilitator and that the Holy Spirit (the Spirit of truth) would guide me and the others in the group.

The primary challenge seemed to be to encourage everyone to take responsibility for where they were in life. To accept that the "bridge of transition" they were on was uniquely theirs. Most importantly, I encouraged them to avoid speaking Greek and to express their experience in a way that empowered them and honored their life path. For most, this included accepting deep regrets about not having been truthful with others and themselves in their past. It was not easy work.

One evening as I invited people to share their feelings with the group, Trina, the 40-year-old woman, blurted out, "Divorce is awful. God never wants us to be divorced. It should never happen to anyone." Certainly her words carried some truth, but her tone and style were preachy and rigid. I encouraged her to speak for herself, owning the experience.

"Can you say how the experience has been for you, and how you have felt?" I said.

She took a moment before personalizing her truth. "Divorce has been horrible for me. I feel sad and depressed about it. I hurt all the time. Nothing prepared me for the pain I would feel." She began to cry as she spoke.

Trina's bold sharing freed up others to share their experiences without fear of being judged.

Sam spoke up. "I'm sorry for your situation, Trina," he said. "But that's not the way it is for me at all. I'm glad to be separated from my wife, even though I am also sad for us and our children. My wife was unfaithful to me repeatedly, and I just couldn't go on living like that. I regret not having been more honest with myself and her sooner."

From that night on we practiced taking responsibility for our unique feelings and situations. We spoke from our own perspective rather than telling others "how it is." We practiced these valuable skills:

- sharing what we felt and thought
- speaking from a position of vulnerability
- digging deeper into the feelings below our surface feelings

- not telling others how things should be
- not telling others what to think or believe
- learning to ask for exactly what we need

Preferences

Speaking Greek often includes refusing to live presently. It is a habit of taking the easy path of expecting others to read your mind, of expecting others to know what you intend without being specific, of expecting that you do not need to know what is important to you. In short, speaking Greek is like slurring your speech. Enunciating clearly takes work, and so does stating what you mean, what you want, and what is important to you. Anything less makes communication arduous at best and impossible at worst.

Speaking Greek is also antithetical to the Scriptures, which encourage us to be truthful with ourselves and others. When Jesus began His ministry, people were not only attracted to His words but angered by them as well.

"'Where did this man get these things?' they asked. 'What's this wisdom that has been given him, that he even does miracles! Isn't this the carpenter? Isn't this Mary's son and the brother of James, Joseph, Judas and Simon? Aren't his sisters here with us?' And they took offense at him" (Mark 6:2-3).

There is no virtue in holding onto our thoughts until they fester into a grudge. Yes, we are to season our speech with gentleness, but we also need to "speak the truth in love."

I worked with Kendra and Kevin for months, practicing the skills I have described in this chapter. After weeks of counseling and hours of practice at home, Kendra learned to be more honest with Kevin. Through our "digging deeper" exercise, Kendra discovered she was not so upset about Kevin's spending as she was with the feeling that she was being left out of his life. She felt abandoned. She wanted him to spend more time with her and to use their financial resources to create exciting getaways for them.

Consider how difficult it was for Kendra to say, "I feel sad when you spend so much time away from home, and I want you to spend more time with me doing special things. I miss the times when we would pack up our things on a moment's notice and head to the beach. I want surprise and joy back in our marriage. Will you join me in creating that?"

Notice the immediacy of this language, the specific requests, and Kendra's willingness to put energy into the marriage. What a compliment to her man! Couples who learn to speak like this can experience new life in their marriages.

Although Kevin wasn't thrilled with her proposal, he warmed to it. He cared deeply for Kendra and wanted to enrich their marriage. Together they learned to share their feelings and preferences without judging one another. Kendra practiced accepting Kevin's enjoyment of his toys without criticizing it. She also practiced asking for exactly what she needed. He still has his toys, but they have begun traveling together more frequently.

Kevin has since learned to listen much more effectively to Kendra. Even when she struggles to say what she wants to say, he practices setting aside his agenda so that he can truly tune in to her. Obviously, this makes her feel great. Although a little Greek occasionally spills into their relationship, straight-talking English is their new language of choice.

Chapter Five

Stop Playing God:
Arrogance Has No Place in Marriage

*True love and prayer are learned in the moment when prayer
has become impossible and the heart has turned to stone.*

—THOMAS MERTON

He was a monster of a man, strutting his stuff in front of the cameras. His mammoth frame took up most of the television screen.

"I was made for this!" he shouted. I felt my skin grow cold. Taunting players on the opposing team, he continued. "I live for this. You're mine." He tapped on his chest to reinforce his sense of domination.

I could have imagined this outrageous display of bravado in the wacky world of professional wrestling—in fact, we expect it there. But I was surprised—shocked even—to see it in pro football. But I suppose *Monday Night Football* is not the place to go if you're searching for humility. As the evening progressed, the game between the Kansas City Chiefs and Baltimore Ravens seemed more a battle of egos than athleticism.

To sensationalize the contest to an even greater degree, the networks have added a new twist. They mike the most bombastic, pompous showboats so that viewers can eavesdrop on them in the huddle, on the sidelines, and in the midst of the action. The end result is a monumental exercise in ego.

Before female readers nod their heads in agreement, a variation of this behavior can be observed in women. On a recent trip to an upscale department store, I observed two women in the mid-thirties trying on expensive clothing as I passed through the women's section.

"Ooh. You look hot in that one," the first woman gushed.

"You think so?" the other said, giggling.

"Check yourself out," the first woman said, pointing to a nearby mirror. "You have got to get that dress. You look fabulous in red—so slender and sexy."

"I love the color. Maybe I'll splurge and get it."

I didn't want to rain on anyone's parade, but I was not convinced the woman in red looked hot. The dress was boxy and poorly tailored.

Warm, yes. But hot? The women were having fun, primping, admiring one another's choices and soaking up the positive strokes. They were not the least bit interested in outside opinions.

Let me offer a personal observation of my own ego in action.

On a trip to Europe last year, I used frequent flier miles to bump myself up to first class. What an experience. At each leg of the journey, I was invited into the Admirals Club. I'm a mere peon. I have no rank at all. But to be served a 12-course meal *before* the plane even left the ground was a heady experience. Attendants opened doors for me, provided steamed towels before and after every meal, and offered me slippers, making me feel as if I were a VIP. I found myself thinking, *I could get used to this. Maybe I am all that and a bag of Snickers too.*

If you are familiar with air travel, you know that the airlines always seat first-class passengers first. Subtly at first, and later not so humbly, I began to carry myself with a swagger as I sauntered to the head of the line. I strode confidently to the ticket taker as if I had done this a million times before. *Yes,* I thought to myself as I scanned the other, less fortunate travelers, *I am a first-class passenger, and I will be seated before you.*

I felt some ambivalence, however. I didn't want anyone to take special notice of me, but I wanted *everyone* to notice. I was in first class, and that brought me power. I was no different from others, yet I was miles (frequent flyer miles, to be exact) above the rest of the crowd.

In every instance, we see egos, alive and well.

And what does all of this have to do with relationships, you wonder? Our fifth critical mistake has everything to do with taking yourself too seriously and relating to others in an egocentric way. It has to do with treating your mate as if you were God.

Consider the egotistical athlete on the playing field, the women in the department store, or yours truly flying high in first class. Do people leave those attitudes on the field, in the store, or at the airport terminal? Too often, they bring them into the home and into the marriage.

How easily these gloating, self-satisfied behaviors seep into the way we talk to our mates. How easily we believe we have a corner on truth. "My way or the highway" becomes our refrain.

Dan and Meg—Playing God

Dan and Meg came for counseling after they experienced a crisis in their marriage and their pastor referred them to me. Meg had decided to move out because she felt smothered by Dan. He had not objected to her moving out because he felt controlled and overwhelmed by her demands. Both had sought counsel from the pastor, who then suggested professional help.

As is the case with many people, their immediate crisis was only the tip of a very large iceberg. More problems were buried deeper in their relationship, many resulting from their attempts to "play God" with one another.

Dan and Meg were high school sweethearts—young, naive, and full of themselves. They were the classic couple—attractive cheerleader and dashing football star. They had endured some rough spots along the way, but they knew they wanted to be together and married soon after graduation.

Dan's father owned an electrical supply outlet, and Dan worked there throughout high school. His job was secure, he made good money, and he was on a fast track to material success. Meg worked part-time as a dental assistant and was studying to become a dental hygienist. She too was goal-directed and destined for success. Both were strong, verbal, and determined—qualities that could serve them well, if reconciled with their relationship. Otherwise, this dogged determination that included a corner on truth could ruin their nascent marriage.

Although earning money was not an issue, being responsible with it was a serious problem. Both Dan and Meg liked nice things, and their debt quickly outpaced their income. Their Nordstrom bill, payments on new cars for each of them, and other credit card debt had put them on a treadmill of trying to catch up to their financial outlay. Both were concerned about their spending, but neither had made the decision to change things. Both pointed the finger of blame. Dan blamed Meg for her clothes shopping; she blamed him for his accessories for his truck. Their relationship had a constant undercurrent of tension about meeting their bills.

Dan and Meg also had a history of arguing fiercely about each other's friends. Dan didn't care for Meg's friends because they seemed "showy" to him. He thought they could influence Meg in some "wrong ways." They were single and wanted her to go out with them for an occasional drink, and Dan implied that they might sway Meg to cheat on him. Meg thought Dan's friends were far too demanding of his time, and she feared they would lead him into destructive activities like excessive alcohol use, which had been an issue earlier in their dating life.

When I met with Dan and Meg, I quickly saw that both were very immature. Dan made snide comments about Meg, and Meg returned the favor. They tended to nitpick with one another, using sarcasm to make their points. When one attacked, the other quickly fought back. This destructive interaction prompted Meg to move out and get her own apartment.

"So, tell me what led to your moving out, Meg," I said.

"It's no fun being married to Dan anymore. He tells me what to do, what to think, how to spend money, and who my friends should be. I can't stand it. When I try to talk to him about our problems, everything is my fault."

"Well, someone has to point out the mistakes you're making. You spend money like it was going out of style—on stupid things. And your friends are trouble, as far as I'm concerned."

"But yours are a lot better, right, Dan?" Meg retorted. "And you seem to forget that you spend money just as much as I do."

"Not like you, that's for sure. And," he said, turning to me, "you ought to hear what she says about my friends."

"They're all a bunch of losers. You can't deny that."

"See what I mean?" Dan said. "She dishes it out, but she can't take it."

"Hold it for a minute," I said. "Why are you here, anyway? Are you really interested in working on your marriage?"

Meg looked over at Dan, then back at me.

"I'm not sure. He makes me so mad. He acts mean and then quotes Scripture at me—'the man is the head of the house' stuff. I hate it. But we really did have something wonderful not that long ago. I do want to get that back."

"How about you, Dan?" I asked.

"Yeah, I still love her. And I don't want a divorce. But man, some things have to change. I hate hearing that my decisions are crazy, that my friends are foolish. I feel boxed into a corner, humiliated, like I'm a bad little boy. I'm supposed to be the man in the house, but not with her, that's for sure."

I spent four or five sessions with Dan and Meg, exploring their relationship. Several themes emerged, traits often associated with "playing God." See if any of them are familiar in your marriage:

- Both talked down to one another rather than addressing each other with respect.

- Both had a tendency to tell the other what to do rather than asking for change.

- Both were very critical of the other and voiced their criticisms often and without restraint.

- Both voiced their opinions as if they were *right*, invariably judging the other and condemning the other's actions.

- Both were defensive about their own actions, rarely admitting when they had done something wrong.

We can see why Meg and Dan would want to escape this kind of tyranny. Why would they want to be in a relationship where they did not feel loved and appreciated? Why would they want to be around someone who told them how to think, feel, and act?

This behavior—the insistence on "playing God"—was tearing away at the fabric of their marriage and is all too common in relationships today.

John Gottman and the
Four Horsemen of the Apocalypse

No, this has nothing to do with an end-times movie. Actually, "The Four Horsemen of the Apocalypse" is a term used by noted University of Washington marriage researcher John Gottman.[1] He found four factors integrally correlated with divorce. They are criticism, contempt, defensiveness, and stonewalling. Criticism and contempt are especially pertinent to our discussion in this chapter.

As we look closely at Dan and Meg's relationship, we see they have grown critical and contemptuous of one another. In their arrogance, by believing they know what is best for the other, they have developed disdain for each other. They are not simply critical about a few issues; they are globally critical. Nothing their partner seems to do is worthy of praise. This combination of factors, Dr. Gottman says, is lethal for a marriage.

Gottman says that sarcasm and cynicism are forms of contempt, as are name-calling, eye rolling, sneering, and hostile humor. "In whatever form, contempt—the worst of the four horsemen—is poisonous to a relationship because it conveys disgust. It's virtually impossible to resolve a problem when your partner is getting the message that you're disgusted with him or her."[2]

Contempt develops gradually in a marital relationship. It rarely just happens. If not corrected, it will have a debilitating effect. However, contempt cannot thrive in a humble heart. It cannot exist when people are trying to live in peace and harmony. Consider what the apostle Paul has to say about humility: "For by the grace given me I say to every one of you: Do not think of yourself more highly than you ought, but rather think of yourself with sober judgment, in accordance with the measure of faith God has given you" (Romans 12:3).

Make no mistake—humility is not an easy quality to come by. In our society, we seem to struggle with either low self-esteem—wondering if we are good enough to sing in the choir—or exaggerated worth—believing we ought to be the first one chosen to fill the vacancy on the elder board. We vacillate between fearing to offer our point of view and believing that our perspective is *the* correct one. Gaining a healthy and accurate opinion of our strengths and weaknesses can be a real challenge. But the Holy Spirit can enlighten us on this most important issue, especially as it pertains to our marriage.

Christ, of course, offers us a glimpse of the perfect balance. Consider that He was God and still did not flaunt His power. That is enough to give us pause. The apostle Paul challenges us, "Make my joy complete by being like-minded, having the same love, being one in spirit and purpose...in humility consider others better than yourselves" (Philippians 2:2-3). He exhorts us to have the same attitude as Christ...

> Who, being in very nature God,
> did not consider equality with God
> something to be grasped,
> but made himself nothing,
> taking the very nature of a servant,
> being made in human likeness.
> And being found in appearance as a man,
> he humbled himself and became obedient to death—
> even death on a cross! (Philippians 2:6-8).

Violation of Boundaries

As we examine Dan and Meg's marriage, we observe many problems, including issues with criticism and contempt. The most pronounced in my work with them, however, was their lack of boundaries. Healthy boundaries would prevent these hurtful behaviors:

- Dan was telling Meg what she was thinking (and vice versa).

- Meg was telling Dan what he "should" and "should not" do (and vice versa).

- They were giving unwanted opinions.

- They were labeling each other's actions as "right" or "wrong."

- They were blaming each other for the problems in their marriage.

As I worked with Dan and Meg, I found they had no sense that what they were doing was so destructive. They had never taken a reflective step back and considered what they were doing to the marriage. They had never taken a moment to ask themselves what they were like to live with. They had never questioned being presumptuous enough to point out each other's wrongs.

Boundaries, as I discussed at length in my previous book *When Pleasing Others Is Hurting You,* determine what is my responsibility and what is not. They show what I can change, what is my responsibility to change, and what is not. Dan and Meg had no understanding of these concepts, and one of our first steps in counseling was to determine healthy boundaries.

All healthy relationships are built on the foundation of healthy boundaries. The first step is to acknowledge that although two people may be married, they are not identical people. They think different thoughts, feel different feelings, and enjoy different things. People in healthy relationships accept these facts. Carmen Renee Berry and Tamara Traeder, in their book *Girlfriends,* note, "All healthy friendships operate within boundaries mutually agreed upon by both parties. Occasionally, one friend will find it necessary to set limits for herself that may feel uncomfortable, or even painful to the other."[3]

Dan and Meg slowly began to see that telling the other what they should and should not do could be very demeaning. They learned that when they rigidly maintained a position on a topic and proceeded to tell the other that he or she was "wrong," they eroded their love. They were making each other feel small, and this never helps a relationship.

Living in Opposition

We may enjoy watching players match brawn and bravado on the football field or engage in a discussion of creative possibilities in the workplace, but living in continuous opposition with your mate takes a tremendous toll on your marriage. And living in opposition begins with attitudes that can often reveal that someone is playing God.

Consider a lonely man named Bert who has only a vague awareness of his oppositional attitudes. Now in his early seventies, Bert lives alone. He is a rumpled man with an unruly gray beard. His clothes are weathered and stained and carry the dense odor of smoke. His fingernails are stained yellow from tobacco. Bert has an unusual lack of pretense, calling a spade a spade and caring little about the impact of his words.

Bert came to see me for symptoms of severe depression. He groused about having to see a "shrink" and was clearly coming with more than a little reluctance—he felt that he had no other recourse to battle his sagging mood. He had been overwhelmed by an abiding sadness since his last wife left him several years ago, in large part due to his intolerance. He had no friends and only occasionally attended church, which was his only outlet for social support.

Today, he still finds fault with his ex-wife, obsessing about her shortcomings before admitting that he misses her. He wonders why no one wants anything to do with him. Bitterness seeps out of every pore. He broods about his children failing to call. He spends his days watching soap operas and counting school buses as they drive by his dimly lit home. The daily newspaper is his only connection to the outside world. Not surprisingly, he even finds fault with "the daily rag."

To say Bert is hypercritical is like saying it rains a little in Seattle in November. When people do not promptly return his phone calls, they don't care a whit about him. When they forget to thank him, they are ingrates. Others never do enough for him, and yet, amazingly, he cannot see how demanding he is of others and how little he does for anyone else. Bert cannot even enjoy his own company. His behaviors and critical attitude are deeply entrenched, and we both realized that he had a great deal of work to do if he was to find happiness again.

Bert has not always been this way. As he tells it, he had a happy life until adolescence, when his father started drinking and became violent with his mother. The oldest of four children, Bert took the brunt of his father's wrath. He left home as soon as he could to escape this madness, and he joined the Marines. There he learned to become "a lean, mean fighting machine." Not much has changed since. Married several times, he has a history of using alcohol excessively, further exacerbating problems with depression and isolation. He has fought with others in every area of his life.

Bert is able to concede that he can be "a bit difficult and demanding." Reluctantly, he admits that he ran his family like a commanding general. Now, alone and disgusted, he continues to blame others for his problems and will find no relief until he is able to see the role he plays in them. He is locked in a prison of his own making—living in opposition to the world—believing that he is right and the rest of the world is wrong.

In his meager way, Bert reached out to show me he was capable of caring. After hearing me tell him how much I liked lattes, he brought me the most robust latte I've ever had. I smiled politely as the "triple-shot espresso" rushed to my brain. "I like them myself," he said with a grin. I could see a delight in his eyes that had been all but absent. Bert wanted relief—a connection with someone who might understand his dark, lonely, self-absorbed world.

Ironically, Bert's depression may turn out to be his saving grace, for in it he one day may be humbled and decide that he cannot live happily in opposition to others. In his sullen sadness, he may decide that others are not always wrong, that he must make some changes. The keys to his relief are humility and tolerance—the stark realization that he is not God and must give up judging others if he is ever to be happy.

Overfunctioning

Bert is an angry, depressed man. His is one form of our fifth critical mistake. Other forms are a bit subtler. One variation of this theme is *overfunctioning.*

You undoubtedly know someone who acts like Dan or Meg or Bert. Perhaps you can see vestiges of the self-centered, arrogant tyrant in the way you fight at times—albeit with more subtlety. Have you found that you enjoy playing God? Have you been tempted to tell others how to live their lives, as if they were not capable of doing so themselves?

Harriet Goldhor Lerner, author of the *The Dance of Intimacy,* talks about this issue at length. She calls folks with these problems *overfunctioners* and lists a number of traits common to them.

- They know what's best for themselves and for others as well.

- They move in quickly to advise, fix, rescue, and take over when stress arises.

- They have difficulty staying out of other people's issues and allowing them to struggle with their own problems.

- They avoid worrying about their own goals and problems by focusing on the goals and problems of others.

- They have difficulty sharing their own vulnerable, *underfunctioning* side, especially with those people they believe have problems.

- They may appear to be "always reliable" or "always together."

Lerner adds, "If we overfunction, we may truly believe that God is on our side. Surely, we have done everything possible to be helpful and our greatest source of distress is the other person—who is unable or unwilling to shape up."[4]

Having a relative or neighbor with these qualities is one thing, but living with a dominating person is quite another matter. In fact, these qualities are not simply bothersome; they are toxic to the health of a marriage. Consider how you rate on the list above. How easily do you fall into overfunctioning?

Another aspect of overfunctioning involves owning our projections. This means that often, when we are telling others how to live their lives, we are actually acting out some hidden, shadow part of our own life. We dislike in others what we cannot stand in ourselves. We are intolerant of others' traits because those are the very traits of our own that we despise.

Dan, Meg, and Bert were all overfunctioning at times. Whenever they tried to do more than they should, they were overfunctioning. When they did something for people who should have taken care of things themselves, they were overfunctioning. Every time they tried to control another's life—even if their intentions were good—they were overfunctioning.

Stephanie Dowrick, in her book *Forgiveness and Other Acts of Love*, offers this challenge and encouragement:

> Only by risking knowing how complex and contradictory you are, and owning up to who that person is, can you discover that actually you can tolerate your own uncomfortable desires, needs and emotions and no longer need to believe that they are happening elsewhere...Knowing who you are, feeling responsible for who you are and what you do, it is possible to tolerate most of what life brings you, and to feel increasingly confident you can do that.[5]

If we spend more time listening to what is happening inside us and owning the uncomfortable aspects of our nature, we spend less time being critical of others. When we see the plank in our own eye, we aren't so concerned about the speck in someone else's eye. What an empowering concept!

The Power of Pontification

Because presumptive control is so destructive, we must ask ourselves why we find it so appealing. The answer is found in one word: *power.*

Yes, that's right. *Pontificating brings power.* Those who overfunction or act as dictators in their households find some sense of worth in running the show. They see a job that needs to be done and take it upon themselves to ensure that it gets taken care of. The domineering mother or father tells the family how things will be done—and their word is law. People use raw, intoxicating power to fill holes in their souls, the results of damaged self-esteem from earlier years of family turmoil.

Another reason for pontificating is *the childhood role.* Drill sergeants are more often made than born. Many discover early in life that their role in the family will be to care for others. They begin by ordering around younger siblings and progress to ordering around their spouses.

Others have erroneously learned that *the world is black and white, right and wrong.* Many people truly believe there is a right way to do things, and anything else is wrong. People with this narrow view of the world squeeze their spouses into boxes that can be very suffocating. Rigid pontificators may not even be aware they are controlling others with this limited mind-set. Pontificators' worlds are small, and they expect you to conform to it. If you have any doubts about their veracity, they can give you plenty of proofs that support their position!

Finally, *pontificating often elicits a reaction from the other party.* When one person blasts away with their "right" view of the world, the person on the receiving end naturally becomes defensive. Both sides take their positions, build their bunkers, and bring in reinforcements to protect their territory. They reduce their relationships to win-lose battles.

Confronting these different "reasons" for pontificating requires a great deal of maturity. Change starts when we realize that playing God has no place in a vibrant, creative relationship. Understanding and respecting others' boundaries demands strength and humility. It requires that we allow them to change and grow at their own pace. Only with quiet resolve can we let others make their own mistakes and learn from them. We need strength to stand aside and permit others to follow the path of their own choosing. Sometimes, keeping our hands off a situation and simply offering a prayer is more magnanimous than inserting ourselves in another's life in the name of rescue.

Love Is Separateness

Scott Peck shares another perspective on the importance of separateness and individuality in relationships:

> Although the act of nurturing another's spiritual growth has the effect of nurturing one's own, a major characteristic of genuine love is that the distinction between oneself and the other is always maintained and preserved. The genuine lover always perceives the beloved as someone who has a totally separate identity. Moreover, the genuine lover always respects and even encourages this separateness and the unique individuality of the beloved. Failure to perceive and respect this separateness is extremely common, however, and the cause of much mental illness and unnecessary suffering.[6]

Peck goes on to explain that the failure to perceive the separateness of the other is called narcissism—something that both Dan and Meg possessed in large doses. In essence, narcissism says, "You will think like me, be like me, and do what I want you to do." It shows that healthy boundaries do not exist, and it fails to acknowledge others as separate from ourselves. Our spouses are simply extensions of our wills, rather than separate people with separate feelings and thoughts—thoughts and feelings that they understand to be perfectly acceptable.

My practice is made up largely of women who, in one sense or another, have lost their individuality through an insidious process. Consider the woman who grows up expecting to be a mother, a wife, a caretaker. She has been groomed to give, to devote more time to others than to herself. She wants to make her mark in the work world, but she often finds that her caretaking responsibilities sap her lifeblood. Her children expect so much of her; her husband expects even more; her boss wants all of that and then some.

Subtly but incessantly, separateness gives way to exhaustion and discouragement. So many forces tell her how to think, behave, and be. Ultimately, in abject frustration, she may come out swinging.

When we consider the problem in these terms, we can see the destructiveness that lack of separateness has upon a marriage. Yet because of denial, many people like Dan and Meg are trying to assert control while failing to see each other as viable human beings, capable of fully managing their own lives.

The poet Kahlil Gibran wrote about the value of separateness in relationships:

> But let there be spaces in your togetherness,
> And let the winds of the heavens dance between you.
> Love one another, but make not a bond of love;
> Let it rather be a moving sea between the shores of your
>   souls.

Fill each other's cup but drink not from one cup.
Give one another of your bread but eat not from the same
 loaf.
Sing and dance together and be joyous, but let each one of
 you be alone,
Even as the strings of a lute are alone though they quiver
 with the same music.
Give your hearts, but not into each other's keeping.
For only the hand of Life can contain your hearts.
And stand together yet not too near together;
For the pillars of the temple stand apart,
And the oak tree and the cypress grow not in each other's
 shadow.[7]

I was drawn to the work of Kahlil Gibran during the moody, angst-filled years of young adulthood. He had a way of saying things I felt but had no way to express.

I recall reading the words above and feeling befuddled by them. What did he mean when he referred to "spaces in your togetherness"? Now I see the truth in them.

Listen to Peck again as he describes the solitary travels in marriage. "It is the return of the individual to the nurturing marriage or society from the peaks where he or she has traveled alone which serve to elevate that marriage or that society to new heights. In this way individual growth and societal growth are interdependent, but it is always inevitably lonely out on the growing edge."[8]

Solitude

For many people, solitude can be frightening. In fact, some believe it is dangerous to the health of a relationship. I disagree.

Reasonable doses of solitude, like seasonings on a gourmet dish, add to the relationship's flavor and quality.

Anthony Storr, in his groundbreaking work *Solitude*, writes that the ability to be comfortably alone is a sign of maturity. Conversely, a dependence on others is a sign of immaturity. Storr insists that solitude can be a valuable resource. It "enables men and women to get in touch with their deepest feelings, to come to terms with loss, to sort out their ideas, to change attitudes."[9] He likens solitude to dream time—time when we metabolize the challenging events in our lives.

For some people, the idea of being alone is overwhelming. They harbor insecurities that they reinforce by being with their mates, children, or friends at every possible moment. But this enmeshment is not healthy for the people who fear solitude or for the people on whom they rely. We should keep in mind that at times, Christ chose to be utterly alone to ponder His thoughts and feelings and to commune with the Father.

I require a degree of solitude to maintain my emotional well-being. This isn't antisocial behavior; I just need time to collect myself so that I am a healthier and more personable individual. I have more to offer after I have had time to journal and pray. I find that I am more patient with others and feel much less need to fix, control, or manipulate when I have had time to process the stirrings in my heart.

Recently, a friend confronted me about leaving a dinner engagement before some others had left. He felt that I must have been angry or upset about something. After thanking him for his concern, I assured him that I was completely at peace. In fact, I had left the gathering at just the right moment—after I felt comfortably "filled" with good food and conversation. I mentioned that I also wanted to allow some time for solitude later that evening. I said I hoped he would understand and not consider my leaving a personal affront.

My friend's questions suggest that others may not always understand our need to be alone. They may take our love of solitude as a personal rejection, even though it is not. We can do our best to explain, but ultimately, the issue is theirs to resolve.

Avoidant Individualism

When talking about the peril of one behavior, I am aware that readers might believe that I am promoting its opposite. I am not. Extreme behavior, especially when it has to do with the delicate dance of relating, will nearly always land us in trouble.

Many times in my practice, I have witnessed the enmeshment of couples. I have watched people audaciously tell their mates how they should think and behave. This extreme behavior, in the form of violating the other's emotional boundaries, is very destructive. However, I also frequently see the opposite—couples in a "live and let live" kind of existence. This is no marriage as far as I am concerned.

At times, the balance can be hard to find. Consider the spouses who, at the risk of being fair and nonintrusive...

- avoid offering an opinion
- seldom share their feelings
- rarely make a request or demand
- cannot differentiate their beliefs from others
- cannot risk becoming dependent on another person

These traits do not coincide with our definition of healthy intimacy. Rather, these traits fit the individual who wants to maintain a safe distance from any kind of closeness. Overfunctioning may pose its own challenges, but so do the distancing behaviors of avoidant individualists, who are often underfunctioners. Neither path leads us to the hallowed ground of intimacy.

Deferring to One Another in Love

So how do we find the balance? What does it look like? I believe the answer lies, at least in part, in tolerating differences between us and our spouses. We must understand that those differences are what attracted us to them in the first place. By tolerating differences, we are applying the apostle Paul's directive to defer to one another in love.

"Speak to one another with psalms, hymns and spiritual songs. Sing and make music in your heart to the Lord, always giving thanks to God the Father for everything, in the name of our Lord Jesus Christ. Submit to one another out of reverence for Christ" (Ephesians 5:19-21).

This passage has been manhandled badly and is barely recognizable in some interpretations. Many times I have heard people hop-scotch over this passage (called proof texting) in favor of the following verse, which says that wives are to submit to their husbands—that men are the head of the house. But taking this verse in isolation from the previous passage ravages the meaning of the Scripture. We may be tempted to control others, to make them into some kind of image that we fashion. But this type of intolerance is not what Paul is talking about.

Paul's point was that husbands and wives are to mutually submit to one another. They are to be sensitive to one another's needs and do their best to meet them. They are to see their mates as distinct, as separate from themselves, with unique needs. They are not to control or dominate their spouses or tell them how to live.

Neither are they to live entirely separate from their partners. Paul imagined an intimate and holy interaction between husband and wife, where "each one of you also must love his wife as he loves himself, and the wife must respect her husband" (verse 33).

Dan and Meg eventually used this passage to advance their relationship. They avoided criticizing one another and instead practiced encouraging each other. When they wanted a change, they asked for it in a respectful way, allowing the other the freedom to disagree. Instead of telling each other how to live, they practiced seeing the other as a separate, fully functioning adult, even when they did not like the other's actions.

Watching Dan and Meg practice these skills in the context of their specific issues was exciting. Dan revealed that Meg's habit of going out with her friends, in combination with what he considered to be her risqué way of dressing, frightened him. He was eventually able to say this to Meg in a respectful way without impugning her character. More importantly, he spoke to her without demanding that she change. As Dan adjusted his style of communicating, which included owning up to his insecurities, Meg became more willing to limit her outings—much to his delight.

And as Meg became more and more impressed with the changes she observed in Dan, her resentment began to evaporate. She was able to share her fears about Dan's drinking and what she considered to be the questionable character of his friends. Because Dan felt increasing compassion for Meg, he was willing to alter his behavior. Together, this couple developed a win-win moment in their relationship.

In this respectful atmosphere, both Dan and Meg could more easily change their spending and review patterns in their choice of friends. As of this writing, they are considering moving back in together to further work on healthy boundaries in their marriage.

Perhaps Dan and Meg's dance is similar to your own. You must come to grips with the fact that you cannot change your partner. Even as you stand by and watch your spouse do something that annoys the daylights out of you, all you can do is talk about this with him or her. More often than not, this is powerful enough to get the job done.

You must learn to sit with your powerlessness, knowing that you cannot demand that your husband or wife change to suit your desires. You cannot preach or pontificate truths to your mate, as tempting as that might be. Even Jesus honors our individuality and right to accept or reject Him. He gives us the power to choose, and we must do the same. Remind yourself that God is God and you are not—and life is better that way!

Chapter Six

Stop Kicking a Dead Horse:
The Importance of Forgiveness

Weakness is a mighty force in the universe;
let's not throw it away. If you want to convince yourself
of the power of the meek, think about the hold they have on us.
—VERONIQUE VIENNE

I had a somber conversation recently with a middle-aged German man, someone I had met in a class I taught at my church. This stout, balding man came up to me after a class, obviously concerned. We talked about his frustration over the chronic conflict between his three children, ages four, seven, and eleven. Karl and his wife, Gudren, both had thriving professional careers as designers and decided to have children later in life. He told me that he and his wife had not fully calculated the challenges young children would present. Although parenthood provided its share of joy, he made no bones about the drain the situation was having on their marital life.

"Das tropfende wasser hohlt den Stein," he said softly, looking away.

When Karl looked back at me, sadness filled his eyes.

I asked him what he had said. The little German I once knew was now long gone.

He paused, as if regretting having said it. He went on to tell me about a saying in his country: "The dripping water hollows the stone."

I smiled in agreement and told him that I was familiar with a proverb that says essentially the same thing: "A quarrelsome wife is like a constant dripping."

"Oh, no," he said quickly, with apparent consternation. "They are not the same at all. No, not at all."

"Why not?" I asked.

"Being annoyed is one thing, but having your life eaten away is something else altogether."

"Yes," I said. "I see the difference. You and your wife feel your children's fighting takes something away from you?"

"Yes. Especially my wife. And I feel so sorry for her. Our children don't mean to hurt us. But their constant terrorizing of one another steals something from us I fear we cannot replace. Their bickering with each other seems endless. It chips away at our happiness, and we wonder about our decision to have children. It saddens me."

I paused and reflected on his response.

Karl was right. The two sayings were different.

Who hasn't been awakened by the dripping faucet? Who hasn't been annoyed by the creaky door? Yes, these things annoy us. But Karl was describing a situation that went much further. His situation involved the constant irritant of children bickering, but it is similar to spouses chipping away at one another with ongoing criticism.

We are all familiar with the power water can exert over time. It has the capacity to erode the integrity of granite. We notice the smooth stones on the beach, ground down by the washing of the sea. We see where the waterfall has burrowed a path through the rough stone. We see where rivers have carved corridors through mountain ranges.

The critical mistake we will discuss in this chapter is much like the power of water on stone. More than just an irritant, kicking a dead horse—in this case, haranguing your spouse about a well-worn issue—has the power to erode the integrity of a marriage. Insidiously, this destructive energy eats away at a relationship bit by bit, often without notice.

For the next several days, I mulled over the German proverb and its application to marriage. What happens when couples continue bringing up old issues that are best forgotten? Are these conversations more like the nagging woman (or man!)—a source of irritation but relatively harmless to the integrity of the marriage? Or are they more like water on stone over time, eroding the strength and fabric of the relationship? We will be exploring how to tell the difference in your marriage, and what to do about it.

Jean

Jean is a 35-year-old woman who came to see me about an irritating issue in her marriage. An attractive, petite woman, she enjoyed her job as a part-time clerk for a large tire company. Were it not for this one dilemma, her life would be perfect, she said.

"I have a wonderful marriage. Tim and I have been married for 15 years. Great years. I love my husband very much, and he loves me. He's a teacher, so we have lots of time off together. We decided not to have kids and have never really regretted it. We are active in our church, spend our summers traveling, and are quite involved in the community. We have just one problem, and it has gotten larger over time—my husband won't stop nagging me about my smoking."

"So tell me how you have handled it," I said.

"Well, for years he smoked too, so it wasn't a big deal back then. But over the past few years we have both become more health conscious, and two years ago Tim quit smoking. I cut down but haven't quit. I feel terrible about my smoking, so I hide my cigarettes. I know how much he hates it, and I hate it too, but I just haven't been able to quit. I've tried hypnosis, chewing gums, and other programs, but nothing has worked. Now, every time he catches me smoking, we have a huge fight."

"Tell me more, Jean, about why you now hide your smoking if it was something that you used to do openly."

"Tim preaches at me. He clips out newspaper articles on lung cancer and leaves them out for me to read. He points out Scriptures on any topic vaguely related to health, like 'to offer your bodies as living sacrifices.' I hate it, but I probably have it coming."

"Do you really believe that?"

"Yes. I know I should quit. But when he starts lecturing me, I go into hiding mode. I avoid him and cringe when I hear him walk in the door. Then I feel even guiltier. It's gotten so bad that I've started to resent him and myself. He makes comments about my breath and how I smell, and he doesn't like kissing me. It has affected our intimacy."

"Have you done anything to respect his feelings?" I asked.

"Definitely," Jean said. "I don't smoke in the house. I don't smoke in the car. I'm obsessive about washing my clothes so they don't smell like cigarettes. I even use mouthwash before going to bed so that I don't smell like smoke. It doesn't matter. He still makes snide comments—and that turns me off."

"You've asked him to back off?"

"Yes. But he just won't let the issue go. He's made his point. I know what needs to be done, but he keeps bringing it up. Every time he does, I react negatively—yelling back at him, telling him to mind his own business. I want to get back at him. Maybe that's why I still smoke."

Jean and Tim's problem is not unique. Many couples struggle with an issue like Jean's smoking. Perhaps one spouse is angry and nagging the other about spending patterns, choice of friends, or excessive involvement with television. It is not that these issues are insignificant—or that we don't need to set appropriate boundaries in marriage. Many times in my books I have counseled about not walking on eggshells and taking a firm stand. But constant bickering has no benefit. Endless squabbling, combined with ineffective problem solving, tears away at the relationship. Even issues that seem fairly benign can become immensely destructive when we bring them up over and over—kicking a dead horse.

Let's review Jean's dilemma.

- She doesn't like her smoking habit.

- She is respectful of the impact her smoking has on her husband.

- They enjoy an otherwise wonderful marriage.

- Tim is troubled by Jean's smoking.

- He patronizes her about her smoking—lecturing, scolding, preaching, and nagging her about it.

- She responds by feeling even guiltier and angrier, and then she attempts to hide her smoking.

- He becomes even angrier as a result.

- The intimacy in their marriage diminishes.

Jean and Tim have developed a parent-child mode of talking about her smoking. Tim continues kicking the dead horse, causing Jean to feel guilty, resent him, and attempt to hide her habit. Of course this childlike behavior doesn't solve anything, and the problem grows.

You may be tempted to rush to Tim's side in this struggle. Who would want to be married to someone with an annoying habit? I suspect none of us would like that. But Jean has had this habit for the duration of their marriage, and Tim is the one who changed. Furthermore, Jean is respectful of his feelings even if she has not succeeded in giving up the habit.

But rather than rush to Tim's defense, we must look closely at his behavior as well. Although we can empathize with his feelings about her smoking, his actions only make matters worse. He nags Jean about her habit. He displays mistakes we have talked about already in this book, such as pontificating, playing God, and attempting to force his "wisdom" on her. He has told her what he thinks:

- "You have to quit smoking."

- "You are ruining your health."

- "Smoking goes against God's standards for your body."

- "You ought to be ashamed of yourself."

Of course Jean resents this. Kicking a dead horse only adds fuel to their fire. Tim's actions do not help her with her addiction to nicotine. They only serve to make her disappointed with herself and resentful toward him.

How can they emerge from this power struggle with their marriage intact? We shouldn't look for magic bullets, but we can find real answers. Couples can cope with challenges such as Jean and Tim's battle over cigarettes. Let me share the counsel I gave her, hoping she would pass some of it along to him as well.

First, *they must disengage from their power struggle.* Simply put, Tim cannot make her quit smoking. No amount of lecturing, cajoling, guilt-tripping, or persuasive acumen can compel her to change her mind. If it could, it would have done so by now. No, this is her problem, and she must decide what she will do about it. Tim is entitled to his feelings about this issue, and he certainly has the right to determine whatever course of action he deems appropriate for himself. But he will gain no advantage by browbeating Jean with his concerns.

Second, *the power struggle actually reinforces the problem.* Condemning someone for a problem never helps to solve it. A power struggle over a problem just reinforces people's positions. Some amount of rebellion usually sets in. This rarely develops a cooperative spirit. In fact, negative emotion or condemnation actually breeds resentment and has the power to entrench a problem.

I distinctly remember a battle with my father during my adolescence. He insisted that I empty the garbage in a timely manner. However, "timely" on his part did not equate with "timely" on my part. I assured him that I would get around to it. Problem was, I never got around to it. His lecturing and scolding never persuaded me to take out the garbage in a more timely manner Why? Because I had set my mind against him. I was not going to let him win. My issue was similar to the struggle between Jean and Tim.

I recall a situation involving my sons that seems embarrassingly trivial now. But at the time, it seemed like a serious matter.

When my sons were in their teens, they had a habit of wearing my sports socks. I repeatedly asked them not to do this, but try as I might, the pattern continued. No matter how much I scolded them, they always came up with a reason for borrowing my socks.

As I look back on this silly battle, I can see that my yelling and lecturing did absolutely nothing to alter their behavior. If anything, it seemed to reinforce their actions. I transformed the molehill into a mountain. My sons resented me for lecturing them, and I resented them for ignoring what I considered a perfectly reasonable request. Things did not improve until I finally decided the issue was inconsequential and simply let it drop.

Third, *each person needs to truly understand the other's limitations.* Jean was limited in her ability to quit smoking, and Tim was limited in his ability to accept her habit. Each needed to understand and empathize with the other. He desperately wanted her to stop smoking. She wanted to work out the solution to her nicotine habit on her own. Empathy would help them move out of trying to change the other and develop a cooperative relationship. Robert Wicks, in his book *Touching the Holy,* agrees:

> In the process of accepting others' limits and letting go, we must be sensitive to our own sometimes narrow, insensitive belief that only we have the answer to others' questions and life problems...Consequently, humility and patience are watchwords for those who would be caring persons. As we know and have probably experienced ourselves, much harm can inadvertently be done in the name of good.[1]

Fourth, *let go!* Yes, simply let go. Tim needs to quit trying to control Jean. She needs to quit trying to rationalize her habit. All that needs to be said has already been said. Now they just let go and practice the Serenity Prayer:

> God, grant me the serenity to accept the things I cannot change,
> The courage to change the things I can,
> And the wisdom to know the difference.
> —Reinhold Niebuhr

Fifth, *they need to practice setting healthy boundaries in their marriage.* I never counseled Tim directly, but I encouraged Jean to set some healthy boundaries. Tim had the right to his feelings, but he did not have the right to parent her by scolding or lecturing her. She needed to firmly tell Tim that she was not going to hide her activities and that his efforts to control her were counterproductive to a healthy marriage. They would need to negotiate how they would handle her smoking without engaging in immature, power struggles.

Finally, *they must encourage a cooperative attitude toward negotiation with one another.* Couples have faced far greater problems than one partner having an addiction to cigarettes. Was this a serious problem? Yes. Could they discuss it as mature adults? Of course. Could they use their combined spiritual, emotional, and creative energies to work out an agreement? Definitely.

Power and Control

I don't think we can talk about kicking a dead horse without talking about the attitudes that typically underlie this problem: power, control, and intolerance. Why is letting an issue go so difficult? Perhaps we believe that we can dictate the outcome if we simply exert our authority.

Over the years, I have often worked with people involved in domestic violence. This is, as most authorities recognize, a problem of power and control. It is a problem of incredible intolerance. It is often a case of kicking a dead horse. Let me illustrate.

As I facilitate my weekly men's groups, we explore how problems with power and control invade nearly every area of the group members' relationships. Although most of them perceive domestic violence to include hitting, choking, and screaming at their mates, the problem is quite often much more subtle than that and far more pervasive than they know.

Consider Jerry, a middle-aged man who was required to attend my group because he had blocked his wife from leaving their home after an argument. For weeks Jerry defended his actions, saying, "Anyone would do what I did if they lived with what I have lived with. My wife cheated on me a few years ago. She was making excuses for her actions, and it made me mad. She deserved what she got."

Jerry shared that his wife, Barbara, worked at a local grocery store. He wanted her to work to contribute to the family's finances, but he was very jealous of her. Early in their marriage, she had been unfaithful, and he had never forgiven her for it. Now, citing her earlier infidelity, he insisted she "pay for it."

She paid by having to call him if she was going to be more than ten minutes late from work. She paid by having to account for every moment of her time when she went shopping. She paid by having to answer endless questions about the men who came into the store. Jerry dominated every facet of her life.

Of course, this behavior was more than annoying for Barbara. Jerry had been understandably hurt by her actions years earlier, and he had never stopped kicking that dead horse. He gave lip service to having let it go, but clearly his actions contradicted this. He still held a simmering grudge in his heart and carefully nursed the wounds of years gone by. Jerry falsely believed that if he could maintain some semblance of control over his wife, he could "guard against ever being made a fool again."

In his classic book *Caring Enough to Forgive*, David Augsburger talks about the damage that results from holding on to hurts.

> As I remember, recall, review, recycle, rework past experiences, I am holding on to them emotionally even though I know rationally that they are past.
>
> I know that the past exists only in memory and in consequences. Yet in spite of the fact that the memory is only memory, I become emotionally involved with it again as though it were actuality. And instead of accepting the consequences and exploring ways of changing or utilizing them, I refuse them and try to turn time backwards and undo them. Both acts are attempts at holding on to the past and acting as if it were still present. More bluntly, resentment is a bulldog bite that clenches the teeth of memory into the dead past and refuses to let go…

> I *demand* that you turn time backward and undo what
> is already done...I *demand* that you change the unchange-
> able, form what is not yet formed, reform what is already
> formed...I *demand* that you appease, pacify, grovel, suffer
> in atonement for your inability to do the impossible.[2]

Obviously, making these demands in a marriage is ridiculous. We
cannot turn back the hands of time. We cannot reverse harm done to
another. But we can apologize. We can make amends. We can forgive
and move forward—scars, limitations, and all.

Anger

Jerry nurses an enduring, all-consuming grudge. He focuses
obsessively on Barbara's behavior, wrongly believing that he can protect himself from ever being betrayed again. Anyone who has been
betrayed can understand his deep sense of hurt and his desire to
avoid having it happen again. But he is going about things in the
wrong way.

When I asked Jerry if he was angry with Barbara, he denied it.
"No, that was in the past, and I don't think about it now. I just refuse
to be fooled again."

Like anyone with an anger problem, Jerry is focused. He has a narrow vision. He does not recognize that he is consumed by Barbara's
behavior at work, her actions outside of work, her friendships, and
how she talks to others. He exaggerates her behaviors to make them
look worse than they actually are. In short, he is externally oriented—
focused on Barbara while ignoring his part in things—a common
pattern in marriage.

His anger is not generally explosive. Rather, it is a simmering,
brooding, "I won't trust anyone" kind. He has an edge that shows in

his work, at home, and even in his sessions. He has been burned deeply and won't risk being hurt again.

But Jerry's anger is misdirected. Beneath his resentment is an implicit demand and need. If he can understand this need, he can let go of his anger. Jerry can stop punishing Barbara. Likewise, the rest of us can also stop kicking a dead horse.

As I worked with Jerry, I helped him see the unspoken demand in his actions. He was essentially saying, "I can never stand to be betrayed again. I will never to be fooled by anyone. My feelings are too fragile, and I cannot live through another betrayal."

His actions were also punitive and controlling. In essence he was saying, "You have hurt me, and I was innocent. You were bad; I was good. You deserve to be punished, and I will do the punishing. I will constantly remind you of the pain you have caused. You will never live down the harm you have done to me."

When we look at our anger in this light, we can see its folly. We can see its connection with other mistakes we have discussed in this book, such as playing God. We can see Jerry straightening out his halo as he talks about the wrongful actions of his wife while skillfully avoiding the responsibility for his violence against her. We see him vilifying Barbara, exaggerating her mistakes and weaknesses, and casting a blind eye to his wrongdoings. His anger may sound familiar—the product of a deluded mind that attempts to highlight other people's wrongs while minimizing our mistreatment of others.

Marshall Rosenberg, in his book *Nonviolent Communication,* says that someone else's behavior does not cause our anger. Our own thinking does.

> Whenever we are angry, we are fault-finding—we choose to play God by judging or blaming the other person for being wrong or deserving of punishment...At the core of all anger is a need that is not being fulfilled. Thus anger

can be an alarm clock to wake us up—to realize we have a need that is not being met and that we are thinking in a way that makes it unlikely to be met.[3]

Rosenberg offers us some practical examples for looking at how we may use anger inappropriately and how we can learn from our anger.

If someone arrives late for an appointment and we need reassurance that she cares about us, we may feel hurt. If instead, our need is to spend time purposefully and constructively, we may feel frustrated. If, on the other hand, our need is for thirty minutes of quiet solitude, we may be grateful for her tardiness. Thus, it is not the behavior of the other person, but our own need that causes our feeling.[4]

Using Dr. Rosenberg's insights, we see that harboring rage against Barbara for past actions does Jerry little good. It only fuels the embers of hurt inside. Jerry's work is to realize what unmet needs he has. He may need to address issues such as these:

- ❧ grieving the loss of innocence in his marriage
- ❧ exploring ways to create a more dynamic intimacy in his marriage
- ❧ letting go of his need for a foolproof relationship
- ❧ creating ways to build trust in his marriage
- ❧ understanding how his actions are harmful to their relationship
- ❧ discovering how he too has been "unfaithful" by vilifying his wife

Letting go of anger requires that we take a broader perspective. We must move beyond the "You hurt me, and you are the one to blame" position. Letting go of anger requires that we stop focusing on the dead horse and cease wasting our energies kicking it. It requires a decision to move out of the past and into the future. It requires that we understand that kicking the dead horse provides no relief. It only hurts our feet and makes us angrier.

Constructive Anger

You may be squirming, wondering if we sometimes have the right to be angry. What if our spouse is involved in some destructive habit that demands we keep kicking because the horse is not dead? What if an issue is alive and well and demands our attention? That is, in my opinion, an entirely different matter.

Let's say that Jerry is sensing something in Barbara's behavior that exacerbates his feeling of distrust. Perhaps he has never put his finger on it, but in counseling he comes to the realization that Barbara is truly flirtatious though claiming innocence. Here we have a different problem requiring a different solution.

Let's imagine that Barbara enjoys dressing in provocative ways, uses "salty" language, and has male friendships that she maintains through chat rooms. We would be foolish to tell Jerry to let go and simply learn to trust Barbara as she engages in dangerous behavior. In this kind of situation, the couple must be rigorously honest with one another about who owns the problem. Barbara must own her unfaithfulness, while Jerry is responsible for his anger and controlling behavior. Like Tim and Jean, they will need to be clear about what part of the problem is hers—smoking and then hiding her problem—and what part is his—nagging and preaching at her about the problem.

When your anger is constructive, you take responsibility for your part in the problems, and you take action to rid the relationship of them. We must constantly fine-tune healthy relationships, and constructive anger can help us focus on solving problems. Letting issues fester is not good for your marriage or your well-being. Fortunately, Jerry gradually learned the importance of letting go and seeing his part in the problem.

I recall one session in particular when Jerry talked about his past in a different way. He actually allowed himself to fully feel and express the pain of his wife's affair from years ago. Tearfully, he recounted this excruciating season in their marriage. He also acknowledged the role he had played, admitting that he had been difficult to live with and that his attitudes and behaviors had clearly contributed to their problems. For the first time, he took responsibility for his ongoing pattern of controlling behavior and his fear of trusting others.

After cleansing himself with these admissions, he noted that he felt relieved. He said he was ready to feel and trust again. Clearly, Jerry had navigated a critical point in his life. He was prepared to completely forgive his wife for her actions and was willing to do whatever he could to make this happen. He now understood, on a far deeper level than he had previously experienced, that forgiveness is an essential part of healing.

Forgiveness

Forgiveness is a hallmark of Christianity. The gospel story tells us that God offers us the gift of unquestioned forgiveness following repentance for the ways that we have "missed the mark," as incredible as this may seem. Christ remembers our sins no more. Once we realize this and fully integrate this truth into our spirits, we understand that we must do our best to impart this same gift to others. When all is said and done, when a grudge has been nursed long enough, a conversation must come around to the topic of forgiveness, for this is the fountain of healing—for both the giver and receiver.

Any discussion about kicking a dead horse would be woefully incomplete without talking about forgiveness. Who of us cannot relate to this topic? Who has not harbored grudges, lived painfully in the past, and clung to an old issue like a dog with a bone, all the while knowing exactly what we were doing but refusing to stop?

In a recent workshop I gave to a small group of women, we discussed the topic of forgiveness because it is such a vital aspect of well-being. We talked about the importance of not giving power to others to control our moods. Everyone was engaged in the topic and actively agreeing when suddenly a 30-something woman angrily shared her feelings with the group.

"I'm tired of people telling me that I should forgive. I think there are times when you don't have to forgive. I think there are times when you shouldn't just let the past go. I was betrayed, and I'm not about to simply let it go. I can move forward, but I'm not going to forgive."

The woman did not share the specifics of her situation, but the tears in her eyes and the bitterness in her voice were enough to make all of us reflect on betrayals we have experienced. Her clipped words, harsh tone, and heavy sighing said it all: Someone had victimized her, and she was still struggling to cope with her pain.

The room was silent for several moments after she spoke. I was immediately taken back to betrayals I have experienced and others I have perpetrated. I felt the sting of tears well up inside me, and only with effort could I keep my hurt hidden. Suddenly, I was carried back many years when, as a young adult, my best friend violated my trust by cheating with my girlfriend. Our friendship was irreparably broken. I felt the tenderness of my internal scar.

After the brief silence, several women rushed in to offer quick palliative guidance.

"But your anger is only hurting you," one woman offered.

"You have to forgive," another chimed in. "You will feel so much better if you do."

"I know how you feel," a third suggested. "I have been betrayed too, and it's not easy."

When things had settled, I shared my feelings.

"It is very difficult to deal with being betrayed. I can see the sadness in your eyes. I know the sting of betrayal too. The hurt goes very deep, and forgiveness simply is not possible right now. In time, if you choose, forgiveness will be available to you. It will probably come in layers, bits at a time. But only in time and only if you decide that is something you want."

The woman nodded and looked sadly around the room as others shared their agreement.

Let's imagine another scenario: A woman is filled with rage because her unfaithful husband betrayed her. Should she simply greet him at the door and lovingly remind him that all is forgotten? Of course, this would be ridiculous. As clearly as Christ was angered at the moneychangers in the temple and deeply disappointed when Peter betrayed him, this woman would understandably be seriously angered. The rift in their marriage would only heal with time, effort, and divine intervention. We would never expect her to instantly forgive. In fact, instant forgiveness, or "cheap grace," is suspect to say the least.

This woman was not yet ready to forgive, but she would have to take this step in the future. This task faces each of us in some area of our lives. Unless we can forgive, we will keep kicking a dead horse. As Augsberger aptly says, "Forgiveness is letting what was, be gone; what will be, come; what is now, be."[5]

Sometimes, unforgiveness takes the form of openly kicking the dead horse by lecturing on a dead issue. Sometimes, it surfaces in the form of repeated reminders of failures. Sometimes, it prompts sarcastic comments and hurtful jabs.

As is the case of the woman in the group, unforgiveness can eat at a person from the inside out. A constant reminder in the gut says, "I just can't let this go." These nagging thoughts can result in loss of sleep, obsession with the betrayer and his actions, and thoughts of vengeance.

Our hearts have only so much room. We cannot be filled with love and hate at the same time. One will inevitably dominate and expel the other. Likewise, we cannot be stuck in the past while we are moving forward. If we are busy remembering and rehearsing the wrongs we have suffered, we cannot invite new joy into our lives.

One of the most poignant effects of unforgiveness is the wounded person's limited view. When our pain remains front and center, we are unable to acknowledge or appreciate the pain that others are suffering. Similarly, we are unable to understand or celebrate the joys they may be experiencing. In short, our world has become incredibly small, our viewpoint dangerously narrow.

As I consider the issue of forgiveness and reflect on violations and violators in my life, I realize that I am deeply committed to a desire that the world be just. Specifically, I want justice to be done to those who have hurt me. Yes, I'm human—I want revenge. But I am also aware that each moment I spend dwelling on revenge is a moment I do not give to those who are ready and willing to love me right now.

The issue of demands and needs rises again. When we continue to harbor resentment well beyond the natural time of grieving understandable losses, we are held back by our immature demands. We are stuck in demanding the world be different than it is, that our mates be different than they are. And yet letting an issue die is far easier said than done. This difficult act requires supernatural power. God is able to soften our hardened hearts, allowing us to see the fragility of the human condition. He is able to offer us compassion for our wrongs, and in the process, allow us to offer compassion to others for theirs (see 2 Corinthians 1).

The Gospel of Grace

Who among us cannot identify with the woman who wants to extract a pound of flesh from the person who violated her trust? We imagine that perhaps her husband had an affair that broke her heart. Perhaps her best friend revealed confidences to another who broadcast them around town. Whatever the violation, it hurt deeply. And why should she forgive? She deserves to feel righteously indignant.

But that is not where the story ends. Ask the father of the prodigal son if he can relate to betrayal. Consider this story from the gospel of Luke.

In the gospel narrative, we read about a young son who asked for his inheritance. He then went off and "squandered his wealth in wild living" (Luke 15:13). Brennan Manning makes this comment on the story in *The Ragamuffin Gospel:*

> When the prodigal son limped home from his lengthy binge of waste and wandering, boozing and womanizing, his motives were mixed at best…The ragamuffin stomach was not churning with compunction because he had broken his father's heart. He stumbled home simply to survive. His sojourn in a far country had left him bankrupt. The days of wine and roses had left him dazed and disillusioned…Disenchanted with life, the wastrel weaved his way home, not from a burning desire to see his father, but just to stay alive.[6]

Here is where the plot thickens. After the prodigal wasted a good portion of his father's estate, we could well imagine that his father would be less than enthusiastic about seeing his son. He had been horribly betrayed. The father had every right to send his son away.

But that is not what happened. We read this in what Manning describes as the most touching verse in the Bible:

"But while he was still a long way off, his father saw him and was filled with compassion for him; he ran to his son, threw his arms around him and kissed him" (verse 20).

This story, which is a picture of the forgiveness and love God offers us, is difficult to comprehend because it goes against human understanding and human nature. It goes against the way we have been trained to react. His father should have scolded him and asked him to account for the wasted money, we might say. The son should have had to beg for forgiveness before coming into the family home. His father should have drilled him, grilled him, and told him how rotten he was. Then, if the apology was good enough, perhaps some day in the distant future they could forge a relationship again. But that is not the story of the prodigal son, nor is it the story of how Christ treats us. Manning boldly says that this story exemplifies forgiveness actually preceding repentance. This is difficult to imagine.

Kathleen Norris, in her book *Amazing Grace*, describes the Benedictine monastic life. Monks say the Lord's Prayer at least three times a day, continually asking God to forgive us as we forgive others. This is a way to stave off self-righteousness and lovelessness. In a world filled with contention and disharmony, surely we need to strive for a godly love with our mate and others.

Burying the Horse

Let's revisit Tim and Jean and their struggle over her smoking. As of this writing, their marriage is doing well. She still hasn't quit smoking but is looking into new programs to help her stop. It continues to bother Tim, but both have agreed not to get into a power struggle over it. They have decided to handle it in as mature a way as possible. For the time being, Jean will continue to be considerate of his feelings, and they have agreed to create a large enough space for their love for one another to flourish while she deals with her habit. Tim has agreed to bury the horse.

Perhaps, like Tim and Jean, you have an issue in your marriage that keeps resurfacing. Maybe you have become narrow-minded about it, and a bit of self-righteousness has crept in. Left unattended, this can become a cancer on your marriage. However, you can take action and eliminate it from your relationship.

Not only is now the time to stop resending old criticisms and grievances—thereby kicking a dead horse—now is also the time to bury the horse. Consider the opportunity you have to let go of your demand that your spouse change. Consider the opportunity you have to extend grace to him or her for behaviors that have disappointed you.

Remember the grace that God has extended toward you—in spite of your limitations—and give a little back to your spouse. Practice letting old, stale issues die. You'll be glad you did.

Chapter Seven

Stop Living in the Trenches:
Learning to Champion Your Spouse

Being confident of this, that he who began a good work in you will carry it on to completion until the day of Christ Jesus.
—PHILIPPIANS 1:6

I returned recently from a weekend vacation in New England with my son Josh, a 27-year-old medical student in upstate New York. The trip provided a powerful experience in contrasts and a quick lesson in the art of championing a loved one—our focus for this chapter.

After landing at JFK Airport, I waited for a bus in the subfreezing climes of New York City, thankful that I had packed my wool overcoat at the last minute. After sightseeing in the Big Apple for a few hours, I made my way to Grand Central Station—a city within a city where travelers scurried about like ants.

I met my son at the New York Medical College campus, and with Josh driving, we headed for Connecticut. We hoped to catch a glimpse of the lingering autumn colors, investigate a few bed-and-breakfasts, and catch up on each other's lives.

As we eased away from New York, the stale grays of the city gave way to vibrant golds, reds, and greens that painted the undulating hillsides.

Josh and I laughed, shared stories about our lives, and began to talk about where we wanted to stay that evening. As a bed-and-breakfast aficionado, I wanted to gather ideas I might be able to use at my own B and B someday. With suggestions from his friends, we agreed to meander the back roads of New England and stay in two unique places to enhance our experience. They could not have been more disparate.

Our first sojourn was in a charming sea village in Connecticut, and my hopes were high that it would provide an exquisite experience. As we drove down the winding, narrow lane toward Mystic (How could a town with that name not be magical?), masts of sailboats shined in the late-afternoon sun. I felt as if I were in a Norman Rockwell painting.

We drove up to a small, tidy cottage on the edge of the harbor. A vacancy sign in front beckoned us. "Perfect," I thought. Sailboats a stone's throw away, salt air flavoring the breeze, small roads leading back to the town brimming with shops and restaurants. "This is going to be great," I said.

We walked in and saw an elderly man sitting at the front desk. Wearing a stained seaman's cap, faded jeans, and a day's growth of beard, he barely glanced up when we entered.

"Yeah, can I help?" he said brusquely, still failing to acknowledge us with eye contact.

"We'd like a room," I said.

"One hundred dollars. No checks or credit cards. Shirley, show 'em a room."

I hadn't noticed his wife sitting a few feet away. Obviously stocky, with a sullen appearance, wearing a large knit sweater and plaid pants, she winced at his words.

"They didn't ask to see a room," she said.

"No matter. They'll want to see one. Show 'em."

"We'd like to see the room," I said. "If we want it for two nights, is it the same price?" Big mistake.

Shirley started to answer, but her husband, who later announced that he went by "Captain Charlie," interrupted her.

"Don't want to talk about two nights. Just pay for one. We'll settle up for the second night later if you decide to stay. I can always rent it for twice the price if you don't want it, that's for sure."

He scowled at his wife and then snapped, "So are you going to show them the room?"

Shirley muttered something back at him and then asked us to follow her down the hall to the room. It was simple, dark, and dusty. Charlie continued grousing in the background.

"Don't expect too much. And Shirley, don't forget to show them the towels and television," he added gruffly. She nodded but did not respond.

It was sad to see Charlie treat his wife the way he did. Clearly he was not interested in being the least bit supportive of her.

After paying Charlie for one night, my son and I walked to town, feeling quite annoyed by the encounter.

"The only thing that was missing," Josh offered sarcastically, "was the 'Arghh' of a pirate. I thought Captain Charlie was going to make Shirley walk the plank."

After waking to the noises of other guests and hearing complaints of lukewarm coffee and day-old muffins, we decided to see the town and travel on.

In spite of the severe disappointment about our lodging and our host, Mystic did not disappoint. It had two quaint coffee shops—a basic requirement for any village to be called "charming." We were enthralled by the tall sailing ships in the harbor for some time before we headed for Rhode Island.

We agreed on our second destination the next morning after stopping at a tourist information booth in Port Judith, Rhode Island, within view of the Atlantic Ocean. The sun was bright, not a cloud in the sky, the salt air crisp and cool. I took it as a sign that our luck was about to change.

When we walked into the Rhode Island Visitor's Bureau, an elderly woman greeted us. In her rumpled matching dress and sweater, she reminded me of my high school librarian. She looked over her glasses and, in a soft, sweet voice, asked if she could help us. We told her about our desire for a "quaint bed-and-breakfast."

We watched as she ruffled through her Rolodex, calling one place after another, until finally she looked up, smiling.

"There is one room available at La Cappella, two miles down the road. John will give you a good price—he doesn't want to cook breakfast because it's the end of the season. He's happy to have you if that works for you." We were a bit gun-shy, but after our experience with Captain Charlie we were open to anything within reason.

As we drove up to La Cappella, we noticed an older van in the driveway with a vanity plate that read "Surfin." A man in his late forties or early fifties met us at the door. Despite the chill, John was dressed in shorts and a T-shirt. Long, wavy blond hair framed his smiling face.

"Greetings," he said. "You guys must be the ones from across the country I heard about. You'll find that we have the softest beds in the state, and my wife and I will make sure everything is taken care of during your stay. She's the brains behind the business. I'm just an old surfer who likes to entertain. You'll like it here. I promise."

We already did.

As Josh and I entered the redecorated church-turned-bed-and-breakfast, John's wife, Mary, greeted us warmly. Fresh flowers in a vase sat on the corner table. Bright watercolor paintings adorned the walls.

"There's the woman that keeps this place going," John said. "Anything that goes right is because of her, and anything that goes wrong is undoubtedly my fault."

"He's not so bad," she said, smiling at him. "He'll help you have a great time here in Rhode Island. John knows every nook and cranny in this area. Ask him what you want to see and he'll get you there."

"Thanks," we said in unison.

"Mary will show you to your rooms, and when you're settled I'll go through some places you might want to try for dinner."

Clearly, John had learned to avoid our next critical mistake—failing to champion your spouse. He had discovered the power and importance of supporting Mary—and she had discovered how to champion him. What a contrast between these hosts and Charlie and his wife, Shirley, who remained in the trenches, constantly doing battle with one another.

Far too many couples treat each other as Charlie and Shirley did:

- They talk sharply to one another.
- They take one another for granted.
- They make demands instead of requests.
- They put each other down rather than offering praise.
- They fail to get excited about each other's ideas.
- They forget to champion one another.

Most of us can relate to Charlie and his wife, stuck in the harsh, critical trenches of marital warfare. We know what being taken for granted feels like, and we have failed to champion our spouse at times.

I have found myself in the critical trenches far too often. I have mentioned previously that several years ago, my secretaries took me aside and told me I get so wrapped up in my agenda that I forget to thank them for their hard work. Although I did not like hearing this news, I knew it was true. I did not neglect them because of a sour disposition, like Charlie neglected Shirley, but because of my myopic perspective. Unfortunately, the result was the same—a demoralizing effect on my office staff. I now practice noticing the positive things they do for me and the office every day.

Thankfully, I have several relationships in which I feel championed. One is with my friend Christie. Let me share a discussion we had recently.

I have been a coffee aficionado for some time and hope to open my own coffee shop someday. On a recent business trip, I noticed a public library that had a café inside. This was a brilliant idea, I thought. Books and coffee have always made good company. I was eager to share this idea with Christie, knowing she would listen attentively and offer helpful advice while championing the creativity within me.

"You're not going to believe what I saw today in South Bend," I said excitedly.

"An Open sign?" she said.

"A Library Café sign," I said proudly, as if I had created the idea myself. "Don't you think that's a wonderful concept?"

"I think it is a great idea," she said enthusiastically. "I can hear your wheels spinning. I'll bet you're going to call them and figure out how they did it and how you might be able to do it. Right?"

"Exactly."

Although I don't know how far I will take this idea, I like feeling safe to dream and having someone to champion my ideas.

Safety

What did Christie give me that made me feel so good, and why is it so critical in a relationship?

First and foremost, when we champion people, we offer them the safety to be all they can be. We create an environment in which they are free to think and be themselves.

By encouraging me, Christie was telling me that dreaming is okay. I can express my ideas, strange as some of them are, out loud to her.

Without a safe environment, we will never give our creative genius the room to grow. Ideas can never flourish with a harsh censor in the room.

Consider your relationship with your children. Observe new parents as they gaze intently at their newborn. What do you see? Recently, I watched a young couple with their infant in a busy airport. As their baby lay quiet in the stroller, drooling, slobbering, and looking up at her parents, they smiled back at her, making loving sounds of affection. Others watching this couple were caught up in their delight. Adults were temporarily mesmerized by the infant, giggling with delight.

This couple was conveying these messages to their child:

- You are perfect.
- You are wonderful and delightful.
- You are a joy to us.
- You can be anything you want to be.
- Whatever you do will be fantastic.
- You are beautiful.

Not only do these parents believe their child is perfect, but they will dedicate themselves to ensuring she is protected and safe to develop into whatever God has designed her to be.

What if we could transfer this same delight to our marriages? What if we retained some of the early wonder we had toward our spouses? What if we showed delight when our spouses came home at night?

That behavior is extremely rare, and some people think it's frivolous and childlike. Although it may be somewhat childlike, it is anything but frivolous. In fact, it is *mandatory* for retaining vigor in a marriage.

Safety Lost

Of course, the new parents' promise to love and protect their child may wane as the delightful infant becomes a cantankerous toddler, turns into an awkward seven-year-old, transforms into a testy pre-adolescent, and sets her own course as a rebellious teenager. How things change!

As the child grows and other siblings arrive, parents may unwittingly compromise the nurturing cocoon. Jobs and family obligations distract parents from championing their children. Kids grow into adults who have forgotten (or perhaps never learned) how to champion their mates.

In like manner, the wonder and awe of early courtship gives way to the humdrum, day-in, day-out monotony of married life. You know the feeling. Instead of delighting in your mate as he walks through the door, your mind is on the clothes you need to wash, the kids you need to take to soccer practice, the bills you must pay, and the dinner you have not yet started. Anything and everything preoccupies your mind—except championing your mate. Sharing what is in your heart is difficult in the trenches of everyday life.

You may be surprised to learn that creating safety and championing a mate is often not even a consideration in many marriages. The partners become so focused on their own issues that they forget that creating a safety net is absolutely critical if their relationship is to thrive. A marriage can *exist* without a lot of ingredients, but it requires safety to flourish.

Be a Champ

I clearly remember the phone call from Debbie. She was inquiring about an appointment for herself and her husband, Kerry. During our brief conversation, she said they needed something to bring the spark back to their marriage. She wasn't certain that her husband would agree to attend counseling, but she wanted to know if I would help them if he did.

Several days later, they came in. Kerry was a tall, well-built man with a long, flowing beard. My initial impression was that he would be loud and forceful, so I was surprised by his soft voice and passive manner.

Debbie was a large woman with long blond hair. She wore jeans, tennis shoes, and a sweater. She appeared tense and tenuous.

After the usual exchange of pleasantries, I got things rolling.

"Debbie, when we talked on the phone the other day, you mentioned that you and Kerry need something to bring a spark back to your marriage. Why don't you begin by telling me a bit about your relationship."

"Well, I don't think anything is really wrong with us. At least nothing major. But we don't talk much. I think we are the classic couple that has grown so comfortable together that we don't really know each other real well anymore. I've noticed that we've been doing more criticizing than sharing lately. I can't speak for Kerry, but I think both of us may be getting discouraged about how things are going."

"How about it, Kerry?" I said. "How do you feel about how things are going at this point in your marriage?"

Kerry stroked his beard. "Well," he said slowly, "it can't be all that bad. We've been married 14 years and have two great kids. I work hard and enjoy the chance to play golf. Debbie works and likes to attend quilting parties with her friends."

"So, things are okay as far as you're concerned?"

"From my perspective, yes. But Debbie says she's not happy, and I'm having trouble understanding what she has to complain about. I'm definitely not like the guys I work with who spend every night at a cocktail lounge."

"I don't know how things can be okay," Debbie said, with more than a little edge to her voice. "I've been telling you for months that

I want more from our relationship. I'm tired of you giving me advice about how to take care of the house and discipline the kids. And I've asked for more time with you, but something always comes up."

Kerry stared at Debbie in disbelief. He was visibly annoyed. It took several moments before he could muster a response.

"We talked about this the other evening, and we agreed to spend more time together. I thought that kind of took care of things."

"It was a nice start, Kerry, and I appreciate your willingness to work on things. But I think we're going to need more than time. We need new ideas about how to make our marriage better."

"I don't know why you're so upset," he said. "I think most women would be happy with a man who works hard, stays out of trouble, and is a good father to his children. I get the feeling that you don't appreciate what you've got."

Debbie winced and turned away.

"What's going on for you right now, Debbie?" I asked.

"Well, you heard him. He thinks there's nothing is wrong. If that's the case, I don't see how it's going to be possible for us to make any changes."

"Try to be more specific about what you want," I said.

"We don't say nice things to each other. I can't even think of the last time Kerry had a compliment for me. We never dress up and go out for a nice dinner, just the two of us. We don't smile much, and we rarely laugh together. If I even hint to Kerry that we might be able to do better, he gets angry. I've gotten to the point where I'm not very hopeful that things are ever going to change."

Although Kerry had been reluctant to come to counseling and saw little need for change in their relationship, he agreed to participate in additional sessions. I worked with Kerry and Debbie for several months, helping them to see that what they *were* doing wasn't the problem; it was what they *weren't* doing.

They needed to lessen the criticisms and increase the words of encouragement. They needed to learn the fine art of championing their mate.

I explained to Kerry and Debbie that a marriage is like an old car that requires lots of love and attention. I asked them to imagine a wonderful automobile with lots of character—and with lots of miles.

"This car," I said, "has traveled many roads. In the process, it has taken a few lumps and now needs some restoration. The engine needs to be tuned, and a few dents in the body need to be pounded out. The good news is that if you spend some time maintaining this car, it will regain its beauty and give you many more miles of good service. But if you refuse to put the time and attention into it that it requires, you're going to have a major breakdown on your hands."

I told Kerry and Debbie that they would need to practice championing one another. They could not approach this frivolously. They had to see this as mandatory maintenance. They might greet one another warmly after work, smile at one another as they conversed, and surprise each other with small gifts and tokens of affection. They would need to create their own special language of affection as they learned what made the other feel good. Encouragement would be their starting point.

As I worked with Kerry and Debbie during the next few weeks, progress came slowly but surely. Initially, Kerry was not thrilled about practicing this new language of affection, but—to his credit—he was willing to give it a try. During a later session, he even told me how much he liked "the new Debbie" because she was kind and encouraging to him. Meanwhile, Debbie was excited about the changes Kerry was making to bring new energy to their relationship.

The Power of Discouragement

A dark cloud hangs over a marriage filled with criticism and discouragement. It is like a ceiling—palpable and disquieting—above which the spirit can never rise.

Ben Zander, conductor of the Boston Philharmonic Orchestra and professor of music at the New England Conservatory of Music, as well as coauthor of *The Art of Possibility,* describes a problem among his students. He talks of being discouraged when his students seemed stuck in a rut of performance anxiety, lacking spontaneity, creativity, and playfulness in their music.

Zander shares his dilemma.

"Class after class, the students would be in such a chronic state of anxiety over the measurement of performance that they would be reluctant to take risks with their playing."

I couldn't help but consider this problem's similarity to living in the trenches of marriage—or failing to create a safe environment in which spouses champion their mates. How many couples find themselves bound up with anxiety, afraid that they will suffocate the other's dreams and ideas? In a relationship where discouragement flourishes, creativity dies. In this arid place, love cannot blossom.

Zander noticed the profound impact discouragement and the teachers' criticism had on his students. The years of education had taken their toll. Students had become dulled to their own incredible talents and possibilities. He sensed their dormant genius, stifled by a world that measured achievement by false and arbitrary comparison.

So he began to think outside the box. He imagined a world free from discouragement, and he considered the impact that might have upon the student. He devised a scheme—fairly certain the establishment (the conservatory) would not go for it. But he had to try.

Zander came up with an ingenious idea. He called it "giving an A." At the beginning of the course, he told his students that each would receive an A for the quarter if they satisfied one requirement. They must write a letter, dated three months ahead, stating, "Dear Mr. Zander, I got my A because…"

They could not use words such as "I will," "I hope" or "I intend." Their letter had to place them in the future and, looking back, report all the insights they acquired and milestones they achieved during the quarter. More important than their academic achievements, Zander told his students, was the progress they would make as people.

"I am interested in the attitude, feelings and worldview of that person who will have done all she wished to do or become everything he wanted to be. I want them to fall passionately in love with the person they are describing in the letter."[1]

Cutting-edge thinking? To be sure. And, more importantly, *safe— free from discouragement, full of encouragement.* The results of his experiment were overwhelmingly positive. Students became excited again in learning—not for the grade but for the sheer joy of learning. And for the delight of learning about themselves. They learned to champion their own thinking. They learned to appreciate themselves.

Why was Zander's experiment a huge success? I think it says a great deal about human nature. He removed the threat of being judged and the paralysis that generally accompanies it. He added the element of discovery as the students found unique ways of affirming their own learning. They were able to get rid of the nagging worry about grades and focus on what was truly important.

What could happen if we could work in a similar fashion to eliminate discouragement from marriage relationships? What would happen if we followed Zander's counsel to practice "giving an A" to everyone we meet—including ourselves? I assure you the results would be impressive. We never tire of getting an A.

The Power of Encouragement

If discouragement is deadening, clogging the arteries of marital communication, consider the life-giving force of encouragement— or what Zander calls "giving an A" and I have called "championing your spouse."

Zander shares what "giving an A" might look like in the real world.

It is an enlivening way of approaching people that promises to transform you as well as them. It is a shift in attitude that makes it possible for you to speak freely (safely)
about your own thoughts and feelings while, at the same
time, you support others to be all they dreamed of being.
The practice of *giving an A* transports your relationships
from the world of measurement into the universe of possibility.[2]

In a similar vein, when someone asked Michelangelo how he
could sculpt something as powerfully moving as the statue of David,
he replied that he chipped away at the excess material—all that was
not David—to reveal the work of art within, and the statue appeared.

This concept speaks to the critical message of this chapter—the
importance of calling out all the possibilities that lay dormant, fearful, and silenced within our mates. Each of us carries a bit of
Michelangelo, calling out the work of the Creator and all that lies
between us and living up to our majesty, ridding ourselves of that
"excess material." We walk around encumbered with fear and with a
history of discouragement. Our faint likeness to Christ has been
encrusted with criticism. We long to hear the words again, lost so
long ago in infancy, "You are so special to me."

Who has not been wounded by rejection, criticism, and negativity?
Who has not, in the face of such dismissal, retreated into their shell and
vowed to "never stick my neck out again"? Yet, with support, we are
willing to tackle the world. With encouragement from others and the
whispering hope of the Spirit, we walk confidently as we understand
that through Christ all things are possible (Philippians 4:13). We are
catapulted once again into our capabilities through the power and
person of Christ, who lives within us.

Listen to the words of the psalmist, who provides a glimpse of
how God views us.

"I praise you because I am fearfully and wonderfully made; your works are wonderful, I know that full well. My frame was not hidden from you when I was made in the secret place. When I was woven together in the depths of the earth, your eyes saw my unformed body" (Psalm 139:14-16).

A Matter of Perspective

It is not always easy to see the beauty and majesty in another. Rather than having the "eye of the Creator," we wonder what God was thinking when He created our mate with all his or her flaws. How, we wonder with impertinence, could our partner think as she does? How can he act the way he acts? How, Lord, can she be the way she is? Seeing what others do wrong is far easier than seeing what they do right. Acknowledging what we do wrong is even more difficult.

I have shared my own experience in this regard when raising my two sons. Because of my own perfectionism, when I came home at night I immediately noticed all the things they had left scattered about the house. If you have children, you can surely relate. They were...well, they were children. They often left out baseball gloves, coats, shoes, dirty socks, and all manner of other things. I responded by running the home like a drill sergeant. And so, all too often, when I arrived home after a day at work, my boys, fearing the quick, critical spirit of their father, would hide. Without noticing or intending to do so, I had fallen into the critical mistake we are discussing in this chapter—living in the trenches of criticism and discouragement instead of championing their young spirits.

At some point in this sad drama, I began to realize the error of my ways. But change is never easy. I shared my nasty pattern of behavior with a psychologist friend who recommended that I practice "pattern interruption." He recommended that instead of continuing my ritualized behavior of noticing something wrong whenever I walked in the door, I force myself to say something pleasant. Before I could launch into the tirade that was on the tip of my tongue, I had to engage my boys in amiable conversation, asking them about their day or saying something positive about them. At times, I nearly bloodied my tongue. How I wanted to offer them advice on how they could improve their lives. Oh, how I wanted to offer counsel about how they could be better sons. But my friend said this approach was off limits and unproductive. Fortunately, I listened to him.

An interesting result came from this change. My family actually began to like to see me when I walked in the door. Everyone quit running for their secret hideaway. My sons actually enjoyed being around me! They began to open up to me about exciting things that were happening in their lives. They shared their struggles, knowing I would really listen rather than offer quick solutions from a position of superiority.

Anyone can see which world was better for my sons and for me. I slowly realized an important truth—everything is a matter of perspective. I could make my boys behave but lose their friendship. I could waste my energies making them toe the line, or I could work at winning their hearts. The same principles apply to marriage and other relationships.

A Change of Mind

In their book *When Bad Things Happen to Good Marriages,* authors Les and Leslie Parrott address the central cause of bad attitudes—developing a negative mind-set toward your spouse. Face it. When you have settled into a negative attitude, you are not likely to champion your partner.

Les shares an experience when he went to hear the great Rutgers anthropologist Ashley Montagu. His topic for the day was "psychosclerosis"—*hardening of the attitudes.* Les Parrott explains that one of the insights he garnered from Montagu's speech was the importance of inoculating ourselves against chronic negative attitudes. Parrott recommends the following ways of avoiding this dangerous pitfall in marriage.

First, *look for the positive*. This involves searching for good things about your partner and positive solutions to predicaments. Instead of shifting into the easy, downward spiral—talking and thinking negatively—look for positive solutions and uplifting things to say. Try going for a day and then a week without saying anything critical.

Second, *refuse to be a victim*. The Parrotts say that self-pity is a luxury that no marriage can afford. Instead of shaking your head and dwelling on the fact that your mate snores too loudly, is habitually late, or chews food with his mouth open, make a habit of looking beyond the small issues.

Does that mean that you let go of every issue? Of course not. It simply means that you practice seeing the larger picture and put things in perspective. You decide which problems are truly big enough to make an issue out of them. You carefully and prayerfully choose your battles. Then, on the items that you decide are simply not that important, you add a dollop of positive energy to the complex picture.

Third, *give up grudges*. As we learned in the last chapter, letting go of past grudges and practicing forgiveness is a critical component in any healthy marriage. The Parrotts add, "Nothing keeps good attitudes from emerging more than a good grudge. Bitterness and resentment are the poisons of positive thinking."[3]

Fourth, *give yourself and your marriage some grace*. Many bad habits are like ruts in the road. They are so engrained in the landscape that we barely notice them. But we must practice getting out of those ruts and giving grace to our mate.

To champion your mate is difficult, if not impossible, if your attitude is negative. You will be hard-pressed to find nice things to say if you focus only on the negatives of life—and you can find plenty of them. Anais Nin said it powerfully: "We don't see things as they are, but as we are."

When we wear the blinders of negativity, as I did with my sons for so many years, all we see is darkness. We can never fully appreciate the evanescent sun.

The Blessing

Virginia was a 62-year-old schoolteacher with short, bobbed, graying hair. She was thin and neatly dressed in a stylish skirt and matching sweater. She was prompt for her initial appointment and noted on the intake form that she was coming to see me "because I'm tired all the time."

Virginia denied being depressed, and she had none of the usual symptoms of depression, with the exception of lack of energy. She said her sleep was fitful, that she woke several times each night "with the most horrible dreams you can imagine."

During her first few sessions, Virginia provided details about her life. She was happily married, now, in her third marriage. Her husband, Bradley, was a retired airline pilot, and they enjoyed traveling together. Virginia brightened when she talked about their relationship. "We're very happy, but I still worry that I might mess things up somehow, because my first two marriages didn't go well."

Her first two husbands had been dominating men. "I grew to resent them, but I'm a Christian. I vowed I'd stick with it 'till death do us part,' and I tried my best to make things work."

Virginia looked down, and her voice softened.

"I feel terrible about not being able to truly love them. But I was dying inside."

"You asked for the divorces?" I said.

"Yes," she replied quietly. "I feel guilty about it, but in each case it was the right decision for me. I couldn't breathe in those marriages. Both my husbands were angry men. They drank too much and were always down. I generally enjoy life, but I couldn't when I was with them."

"You felt that you had to leave to regain your happiness?"

"Yes. And I've been able to do it."

"What do you enjoy?" I asked.

"My garden!" she said enthusiastically. "I am a Master Gardener and have won many ribbons for my roses over the years. I have about 40 different varieties, and they take up a lot of my time. I'll bring you a few if you'd like," she said, smiling broadly.

"That would be wonderful," I said. "Tell me more about what you have to do to keep roses healthy and robust."

"Oh, it takes a lot of work, but I get lost in it. It's not a chore. Not at all. You mulch the ground and fertilize appropriately. Make sure they have enough water but not too much. You watch carefully for insects and disease. And you leave the rest to God."

I couldn't help reflecting on the obvious parallel to human life. Under the right conditions we thrive. Under the wrong conditions our growth is stunted, or worse, we flounder and die, both emotionally and spiritually.

"Would it be fair to say, Virginia, that in your first two marriages, your personal garden didn't receive enough of the sunlight, nutrients, and safety needed to thrive? With harsh, critical husbands perhaps you could not be all that you could have been had they provided encouragement and security."

Virginia looked at me for a moment, sadness filling her eyes.

"I never thought of it that way, but you're right. My nightmares are always sad. I wake up crying, never sure what I'm crying about. But I've sure had enough to cry about in my life. It didn't all begin with my husbands. My father was harsh and controlling with me as well. He was angry and controlling with my mom also. I heard him yell at her for years. I haven't had a very safe life."

"Have you ever heard of the book *The Blessing* by Smalley and Trent?"

"No, I don't believe so."

"Their book makes me think of your rose garden. Just as you provide the necessary ingredients for your roses to thrive, Smalley and Trent remind us that we need certain elements to thrive in our relationships. These ingredients may not have been present in your early life at home, and from what you've told me, they weren't present in either of your marriages. Without those ingredients, we cannot thrive. In fact, we can barely survive."

I continued sharing with Virginia important insights from the book, in which Smalley and Trent reintroduce the concept of "the blessing." The Old Testament includes many blessings. In fact, Smalley and Trent say, "Some aspects of this Old Testament blessing were unique to that time. However, the relationship elements of this blessing are still applicable today." In large part, blessings relate directly to the critical concept of *championing our mates.*

Smalley and Trent state, "The presence or absence of these elements can help us determine whether our home is, or our parents' home was, a place of blessing…A study of the blessing always begins in the context of parental acceptance. However, in studying the blessing in the Scriptures, we found its principles can be used in any intimate relationship."[4]

Let's look briefly at five elements of a blessing and why they are so important to championing our spouse.

The first aspect of a blessing is *a meaningful touch.* When Isaac went to bless his son Jacob he said, "Come near and kiss me, my son" (Genesis 27:26 NRSV). With many scriptural blessings, meaningful touch provided the caring background to the words spoken. Meaningful touch, as the study of psychology has found again and again, conveys warmth and acceptance. Researchers have even associated it with physical health.

The second aspect of the blessing is *a spoken message of love and acceptance.* After the honeymoon, many marriage partners take for granted the words of love and acceptance. But we never tire of hearing that we are appreciated and accepted for who we are.

Meaningful touch and a spoken message lead to the third element: *the words of high value.* In Hebrew, the word *bless* literally means "to bow the knee." When we bring this blessing into our marriages, we verbally show that our mate is valuable and has redeeming qualities. Some might say that verbalizing these sentiments is unnecessary. "She knows I love her," one man told me recently. "Why do I have to keep telling her?" The answer is that we need ongoing verbal and nonverbal demonstrations of blessing. It is the sunshine, weeding, mulching, and watering that makes the garden grow. Without constant attention, as Virginia found with her garden, the whole thing would go to seed.

A fourth element of the blessing is *the way it pictures a special future for the person receiving the blessing.* Isaac says to his son, "May God give you of the dew of heaven, and of the fatness of the earth... May peoples serve you, and nations bow down to you" (Genesis 27:28-29 NASB). We have a unique opportunity in marriage to picture a special future for our spouse.

Finally, the last element in the blessing pictures *the responsibility that goes with giving the blessing.* Here we offer our mate a commitment to do everything possible to help the blessing bear fruit. Just as Virginia studiously provided the ingredients for her precious roses, we now dedicate ourselves to providing the five ingredients for our beloved. We supply meaningful touch and a spoken message, we attach high value to the one being blessed and picture a special future for him or her, and we confirm the blessing by an active commitment.

In this environment, marriage thrives. Without it, marriage wilts and dies.

Consider how these five elements of a blessing may have existed in your early family life or are present in your marriage today. Thankfully, I read Smalley and Trent's book while my sons were still quite young. I made a deliberate effort to speak these blessings into their lives.

I distinctly remember taking my oldest son, Josh, aside when he was ten or eleven years old. I told him I could sense his gentle heart and desire to minister to others. He was kind and thoughtful to his grandparents, always looking for ways to make them feel loved. I am not surprised that today he is a gentle young man, ready to minister physically and spiritually to those in distress.

As we talked, Virginia cupped her face in her hands and cried for the child within her that had never been blessed, and for the adult that had never fully received these aspects of blessing. In the weeks that followed, we discussed these issues, took time to understand and grieve her losses, and examined ways she could heal and nurture herself and her relationship with her new husband. We explored how God could, even at this stage, reach into her heart and heal past wounds. How God, the ideal Healer, had lofty goals for her, dreamed big dreams for her, and cared for her with an everlasting love, regardless of what she did or did not do to earn that love.

Consider the words of the prophet Jeremiah: "'For I know the plans I have for you,' declares the LORD, 'plans to prosper you and not to harm you, plans to give you hope and a future'" (Jeremiah 29:11).

Benediction

The apostle Paul began many of his letters with words of encouragement. Although he often offered critical counsel, he generously peppered his words with affirmation. Did he know what we know—

that constant criticism only discourages and rarely edifies? That individuals and marriages need blessing and encouragement to thrive? That one doesn't need to earn a blessing? Listen to his parting statement to the church in Thessalonica:

> May God himself, the God of peace, sanctify you through and through. May your whole spirit, soul and body be kept blameless at the coming of our Lord Jesus Christ. The one who calls you is faithful and he will do it (1 Thessalonians 5:23-24).

I always look forward to the benediction after the sermon at our church. I may be passionately moved by the singing and worship and convicted by the preaching and reading of the Word, but I am anxious for the "feel-good ending" of the benediction. Here, in these few quiet moments, my thirsty soul soaks up the words. Here too I wrestle with my qualifications for receiving the blessing. Am I worthy enough? Was I good enough this past week? I do my best to silence the inner critics and simply receive the gift—the blessing.

I was so moved by a benediction given several years ago by my cousin-pastor, Jim Sundholm, that after listening to a recording of his sermon again, I decided to memorize it. I have used it in my workshops to bring our time to a close while offering a blessing to the participants. I offer it here as both encouragement to you and a close to our chapter.

> Grace and peace to you from God our Father, through our Lord Jesus, the Christ, in whom we have all that we are and all that we will ever be, in a world which through God's grace shall have no ending. Amen.

Chapter Eight

Stop Living with Paper Fences:
Learning to Create Healthy Boundaries

Ideally, both members of a couple in love
free each other to new and different worlds.
—Anne Morrow Lindbergh

A cold, crystalline shell clings to my car windows these mornings, forcing me to spend extra minutes scraping and scratching at my windshield before I can leave for work. A full moon the night before means an even thicker layer of frost the following morning.

No more running out to get the paper in bare feet. No more dodging to the car in my T-shirt. I have put away my summer jacket and replaced it with my heavy wool overcoat. Summer is gone, fall is here, and winter cannot be far behind.

Fall invariably turns our focus to issues other than beach trips and barbecues—two of utmost importance: The holidays are coming, and our families will be gathering.

Don't get me wrong. I'm a traditionalist. I enjoy the festivities that accompany the holidays. I like Thanksgiving celebrations, the turkey and mashed potatoes and good conversations. I like having family members arrive from out of town and continuing long-held

155

traditions. I like the laughter and gaiety that have been a part of my family for many years. I love all the reasons for the season.

But make no mistake about it, the holidays, more than any other moment of the year, are the time to practice the key point of this chapter—*learning to create healthy boundaries.*

Holidays are a time when family and friends seem to crowd in on us. Some will test our spirits. All, including our spouses, may stir up issues with boundaries.

I grew up in a large family in a small town on a quiet street. I have three sisters and one brother, and I am smack dab in the middle of the bunch. All of us, including our spouses, children, parents, and friends, will gather for the holidays.

My family, perhaps like yours, comes with baggage. *Gasp!* More precisely, it comes with tendencies to step across emotional boundaries. My family members, perhaps like yours, come with personalities and opinions they are not afraid to share. Some of them are soft-spoken, gentle, and very sensitive to others' feelings. Others are…well, a bit more dominant. Most respect each other's boundaries, but some are less likely to practice this concept. I have learned that any gathering of family and friends brings the potential for hurt feelings.

At a recent family gathering, I experienced a struggle with boundaries. It happened over an innocuous issue, as is so often the case, and began with a simple question.

My father asked how my travels to promote my most recent book were going. He seemed genuinely interested and concerned. No problem thus far. Then one of my sisters (name withheld out of concern for self-preservation) asked if I had been eating right. Uh-oh.

"What do you mean?" I asked.

"Well, you have to make sure not to eat after nine o'clock because your body can't metabolize food as well after that time. It can cause you to gain weight."

I was immediately annoyed. The last thing I wanted to talk about was my weight.

"I eat the best I can when I travel," I said. "Besides, I'm not sure you're right about eating after nine."

By now, I was tense and eager to change the subject. I sensed myself getting drawn into a debate I was too tired to have. My boundaries felt incredibly vulnerable.

"She's right, David," another sibling interjected. "Studies show that you shouldn't eat right before bed because your body shuts down. You have to make sure you eat at the normal time. You should always avoid eating in your room at night. Have you gained any weight while traveling?"

At that point, my father jumped into the discussion. While dear to me, he still tends to patronize his children. I squirmed, wondering what kind of lecture might follow.

"I think it's true, Son. When I was your age I used to come home from working late and your mother would fix me a meal—meat, potatoes, the works—and I gained 20 pounds in a year."

"More than that, dear," my mother said, unaware of my growing tension.

"Okay, 30 pounds. Anyway, Son, you have to watch how you eat when you're traveling or you'll look like me."

At that point, I wasn't sure if I should explain that eating spuds and steak, regardless of the time of day, without exercise, is sure to result in weight gain. I was convinced that Dad's weight gain had less to do with *when* he ate than with *what* he ate. But that was not the issue. And, more importantly, that was not *my* problem. All I wanted was to escape from this discussion!

As you reflect upon this seemingly benign family conversation, you'll notice several things. You'll see that it began innocently enough and ended with me feeling confused and annoyed. You may even smile with insightful understanding, noting that such conversations happen often within marriages and family relationships, perhaps your own.

Let's look more closely. Where did the problem begin? Why did it occur?

My father asked me innocently enough about my travels. No problem to that point. But then I was *told* to watch how I was eating. Although this did not constitute a major problem, I did not ask for the advice. Thus, it crossed the imaginary boundary we must respect with one another. Then, you'll notice I made a mistake—I defended myself. Offering defensive explanations typically only adds to a boundary problem. It sends a message that we are willing, and in fact eager, to continue the discussion, regardless of our discomfort. Before I knew what was happening, my family had drawn me into a discussion about *my weight*—a discussion I did not care to have. Before I knew it, I felt distrustful, irritated, and unsure of myself. I wanted to push away from my family—the very people I care most about and choose to spend time with.

These conversations can occur easily, creating confrontation and anxiety in families and marriages. These are the problems we will learn about in this chapter so that we can avoid making our next critical mistake—*living with paper fences.*

Fences

People talk a lot these days about boundaries, and rightly so. They separate our lives from the lives of others. They define how we are different from others and how we want to be treated. These invisible fences, like the visible ones around our houses, protect us. We are responsible to take care of what lies behind those fences, including our very selves.

Not long ago I wrote an entire book on this topic: *When Pleasing Others Is Hurting You.* I noted that God established the universe with a certain order and specific boundaries. After designing an orderly universe, with water and land confined to certain boundaries, God established a creation that would follow certain physical laws, such as gravity. He also established spiritual guidelines that impact our lives, such as the law of reaping and sowing, which we have all experienced.

Just as geographic boundaries help us define where our property begins and ends, emotional, spiritual, and physical boundaries help us determine what things are and are not our responsibility.

Using this simple definition—*understanding what is and what is not our responsibility, and living accordingly*—the dinner conversation with my family takes on new meaning. Reviewing the situation, we see that my family, though well-intentioned, was violating the lines of responsibility. They were offering unsolicited advice about how I *should* eat. They apparently felt justified in offering this advice because I was their brother or son.

You will rightly note that I am responsible for my part in these family dynamics. I did not set a boundary that let my siblings and my father know that I could take care of myself. Instead, I did the all-American thing—I got annoyed and reacted defensively. Once they hooked me, I tacitly agreed to join in the game.

Thankfully, my family is reasonably healthy. The above scenario is true, but it is neither typical nor particularly serious. Many families act out these patterns over and over on a far larger scale. In these instances, we should not be surprised that family members become isolated from one another. No wonder married couples develop conflicts over boundaries. Families and couples with unhealthy boundaries have these characteristics:

- They have not determined what they are responsible for and what is none of their business.

- They are not able to clearly differentiate what they are feeling from what other family members are feeling.

    They are not able to decide for themselves what they want or what other people want from them.[1]

The anecdote about my family may remind you of a similar situation that has occurred with your spouse or your family. Perhaps you are living with a spouse or family members who offer unsolicited advice too freely. Perhaps you have trouble telling them that you would rather not receive that advice. If this fits one of your relationships, this chapter will be helpful to you.

Two Different Women

They were two very different women. One was tall and slender, the other short and stocky. One had an advanced college degree; the other had barely managed to earn a high school diploma. One was gloomy and discouraged; the other was buoyant and lively. One had boundaries that seemed to shift with the wind; the other had boundaries that were firm and constant. One seemed a bit befuddled; the other had a unique clarity and quickness of mind. These women provided me with real-life illustrations of boundaries and the impact they could have on one's life. They offered examples of the importance of avoiding this critical mistake—living with paper fences.

Kate was a devout Christian woman in her fifties who came to see me for symptoms of depression. Dressed perfectly in matching blouse and skirt, her gray hair neatly styled, she had been struggling with low energy and a lack of enthusiasm for several years. She told me that her friends thought of her as "sweet as honey," but Kate wondered if any of them really knew her. Odd as it may seem, Kate's trouble stemmed from her obsession with not hurting anyone's feelings.

"It's the way I was raised," she said. "My mom taught me never to talk back to anyone. She said I should always put others' needs above my own. That's the way she lived her life."

Kate offered an occasional smile when referring to herself as "a proud Southern woman. I respect other people, and I expect them to respect me. We Southerners don't demand our own way. We try to show class, not arrogance. More than anything else, we want to be hospitable. That's just part of who I am. We were taught from early on to take care of others."

"You never put yourself first, and you always make others comfortable before yourself," she said. "It's the right thing to do. It's the way of the Bible."

Kate told me she was married to a "strong, independent man." Now retired, Gene had been a successful businessman, and he demanded a great deal from Kate while giving little in return. For years she had enjoyed the benefits of his six-figure salary. She liked entertaining in their spacious Mediterranean-style home on the hill overlooking the city. She also reveled in the social recognition at the country club. But she didn't enjoy Gene's controlling nature.

Still, Kate wondered why that would make her so irritable. She wondered why his dominance had made her unsure of herself over the years. She gave numerous examples of how he told her what to do, what to think, and how to feel. Yet, surprisingly, not until recently did she recognize this as being inappropriate—even as it took its toll on her self-esteem.

Kate said she had been depressed for several years, especially after her four children left home. She missed her kids and cautiously shared with me that being with her husband had become difficult for her. Because Gene was now retired, he was home far more often and had become increasingly demanding. He wanted to be waited on, entertained, and fed exactly what pleased only him. He was irritable much of the time, which she attempted to ignore and tried to assuage in different ways. But her efforts had not succeeded in warding off her blues.

Recently, two of her children had been quarreling with each other. Both daughters called Kate and sought her support. She had difficulty setting limits on either one and was easily drawn into their conflicts. Each would spend hours talking to Kate about her side of the story. Kate was unsure how to handle it because she empathized with both. Her husband had little sympathy for her plight and encouraged her to "let them fight it out," leaving her feeling even more isolated.

Cynthia was a stunning contrast to Kate. In her early sixties, dressed in a sweater, jeans, and a red beret, she came to see me after her husband of 30 years divorced her for another woman. From the opening greeting she was intermittently tearful, especially when talking about the divorce. It had rocked her world, and she was desperately trying to make sense of things.

But beneath her pain, Cynthia evidenced a quiet strength. She showed a feistiness that surprised me. Clearly shaken by this unwanted situation, she vowed to become even stronger in the process. A firm-minded woman, Cynthia could be bold with a hint of brashness at times. She had a reputation, she proudly told me, for speaking her mind.

Although Cynthia was clearly sad about her incredible loss, she was mostly angry. She was indignant that her husband could "divorce me, our children, and our grandchildren" after developing a life together. These were the years she had hoped to enjoy as a larger family, and now the family was splintered. She was still struggling to "make sense of the whole thing." She had come to counseling, hoping I could help her understand why the divorce had happened, resolve her grief, and move on with her life. After our first meeting, I had little doubt about her ability to accomplish these things.

As Cynthia reflected on her marriage, she shared her embarrassment at tolerating too much "abuse" from her ex-husband over the years. She told me about his history of philandering, and how she had endured it "for the sake of the children." She had repeatedly rescued her husband during his escapades, offering him a warm home where she would "forgive and forget." Now, after all of her sacrifices, she was angry that he had squandered her caretaking and left her for someone else.

When I asked Cynthia why she had put up with this constant disrespect and mistreatment from her husband, she began to realize that she had tolerated far too much. And by doing so, she had only reinforced his irresponsible behavior.

"I kept believing that he would change. I know it sounds silly, but I thought he would grow up one day. I really believed he would find out that the grass isn't always greener and would finally get tired of cheating. I was naive, probably even stupid in some ways. I even secretly believed that God would step in and help me if I kept the faith. But now I understand that God allows people, including my husband, to find their own way, even if it means others get hurt by what they do."

Both Cynthia and Kate struggled with emotional difficulties. Kate suffered from a significant depression; Cynthia had some similar symptoms, but hers stemmed from a transient grief reaction. The prognosis was very different for the two women. With stronger boundaries, Cynthia could expect to rebound from her loss relatively quickly. She looked back and understood how she had allowed her husband to take advantage of her with his affairs. Now, she generally felt in control of her life and vowed to come back stronger than ever. She expected good things for her future.

Kate, on the other hand, would likely have a harder time of it. She had struggled with low self-esteem for years. She had developed troubling traits that might take years to overcome, such as enabling her husband's demanding behaviors. With paper fences for boundaries, her depression was entrenched and would not lessen quickly. She had many skills to learn before she could expect to improve significantly. Learning to create healthy boundaries, however, was important work for both women, and may be an important issue for you as well.

Both Kate and Cynthia struggled to follow the scriptural mandate offered by the apostle Paul in Galatians 6:2,5: "Carry each other's burdens, and in this way you will fulfill the law of Christ…Each one should carry his own load." The word "burden" suggests something that is nearly impossible to manage alone. We are to help others when they encounter some obstacle that is impossible for them to manage. But they are to carry their own "load"—those daily responsibilities in life.

Paul's words are hard for many of us to abide. We are often confused about the best way to care for those we love. We can rationalize our "caretaking" as "caring," and our excessive enabling as loving behavior. Christians in particular may enable others' weaknesses in our desire to be generous people. But too often, we fail to honestly examine how our behavior amplifies and extends problems.

As we review Kate's and Cynthia's lives, we see that both were confused about these issues. Kate overlooked her husband's controlling behavior in return for the fancy home on the hill. She gave far too much in return for far too little, allowing herself to be disrespected again and again. The price she ultimately paid was a loss of self-esteem and eventual depression, all because she made the critical mistake of living with paper fences.

Cynthia had more spunk and showed a strong desire to move out of the role of victim. But she too had allowed her husband to take her for granted. For years, she tolerated the abuse of her husband's philandering in exchange for a seemingly stable family life. Although we can sympathize with her and understand her desire for stability, the price she paid was very high. She carried a burden that was not hers to carry. Her husband's behavior needed attention years ago, and overlooking it did no favors for her, him, or their family.

The Impact of Boundaries

Marriage is difficult. Families have their challenges. However, these troubles afford us a unique opportunity. We must view these predicaments as opportunities for growth. We can learn a lot by noticing the lack of boundaries in my family's interaction and the lives of Kate and Cynthia. The ability to set boundaries is one of the most important tools anyone can learn. If we do not master the skill of setting boundaries, our lives will be in turmoil. Without boundaries we are...

- unsure of what we think
- unable to clearly say what is true for us
- uncertain how our thoughts are different from others' thoughts
- confused about how to take care of ourselves
- troubled about setting limits on some of our behaviors
- frustrated with others taking advantage of us

In contrast, when we learn the fine art of boundary setting, we...

- know what we think
- are able to say yes to good things and no to bad things
- know how to take care of ourselves
- know how our thoughts are different from others' thoughts
- take responsibility for our actions, not the actions of others
- respect others' ability to say yes and no, and honor their decisions
- know how to set limits on others' intrusions into our lives
- know how to set healthy limits on our activities

As you can see, boundaries can bring great freedom. Let's look again at the interaction of my family, this time placing special emphasis on the impact of unclear boundaries.

First, my sister, without any negative intent, asserted that I had to watch how I ate when traveling. Although this may seem innocuous, problems often start with someone telling us what we *have to do*. Few of us want to hear what we *should* be doing unless we have invited that person to speak into our lives.

Second, notice my obvious irritation, a sign of my defensiveness. However, I did not directly attend to my annoyance or use it to set a boundary on this discussion. So things progressed.

Next, another sibling jumped into the mix and reiterated that I must watch what I eat. This gave additional substance to the importance of watching what I eat and the "fact" that weight gain occurs when we eat after nine at night.

Finally, my father added his two cents' worth to the discussion, apparently unaware that my sisters were violating my boundaries. I allowed my entire family to give me a lesson on eating while traveling, but I had no interest in the topic or their opinions regarding it.

Fortunately, this conversation began and ended within minutes and without further incident. However, it could have taken a turn for the worse at any number of points. Thankfully, no one's feelings were hurt, and we moved forward with our family celebration.

But what would have happened if the intensity had increased 10 percent? What if I had been a bit more tired and taken exception to this unsolicited counsel? What if someone had continued telling me how I should eat or mentioned that it appeared I'd gained a few pounds during my travels? Or what if I had decided to set a boundary by announcing that I really didn't want to talk about the subject?

Though these boundaries within my family may seem incredibly trivial, they are anything but that. Some will undoubtedly believe that if I can get my feelings hurt over travel advice, I need to get a life. Quite the contrary. This interaction perfectly illustrates a key point of this chapter: Setting boundaries within our family and marriage keeps relationships healthy. We must be vigilant about "boundary maintenance" if we want to keep our relationships strong and vibrant.

Boundaries in Marriage

If boundaries in families are complicated, what happens to them in marriage? Townsend and Cloud, in their book *Boundaries,* provide us with some insight:

> If there were ever a relationship where boundaries could get confused, it is marriage, where by design husband and wife "become one flesh" (Ephesians 5:31). Boundaries foster separateness. Marriage has as one of its goals the giving up of separateness and becoming, instead of two, one. What a potential state of confusion, especially for someone who does not have clear boundaries to begin with![2]

Townsend and Cloud state that problems arise when we trespass on another's personhood by crossing the line and trying to control another's feelings, attitudes, behaviors, choices, and values. Let's look a bit closer at a few examples.

Feelings

Perhaps nothing is as unique to our individuality as our feelings. I am keenly aware that few people feel about things as I do. I often find that the things I become passionate about are far less significant to others. Conversely, I find that what is important to others may not matter to me at all.

This point was brought to light recently during our national elections. I have always felt that I *should* be passionately involved in politics—yet, for the most part, I am not. During the recent presidential election, many people hotly debated the pros and cons of each of the candidates. I found some aspects of the contest fascinating, but I was more interested in matters that affected me on a day-in and day-out basis, such as writing this book, selling my sailboat so I could buy a bigger one, setting up a party for my business network group, and so on.

Feelings clearly set us apart from each other. They help determine how I will react differently from you on any given topic. They are unique aspects of our personality that can define us far more than hair color, height, or heritage. Problems occur when we try to tell others what they *should* feel. This simply does not work and only serves to create tension in a marriage.

Desires

We need to take responsibility for another key aspect of our personhood: our desires. We each want uniquely different things, and we are responsible to negotiate those in our marriage. Usually, no one person's desires are universally right or the other's universally wrong. They are simply different.

Kate and Gene, from earlier in the chapter, struggled with the issue of desires. Kate was caught in the conflict between their daughters. Kate wanted emotional support and participation from Gene, but Gene did not want to get involved in their daughters' conflict.

I tried to help Kate see Gene's desire not to get involved as his choice—not necessarily as right or wrong. A satisfactory outcome would have been for her to share her desire with him and the two of them to seek a solution to the problem together. Unfortunately, this did not occur.

Limits on What I Can Give

Each of us must decide what we can and cannot give. We must also determine where giving ends and resentment begins. Almost without exception, we feel resentment in a relationship when we have given past our point of comfort. We no longer feel loving about our giving. Instead, we feel resentful.

Kate grew up being a giver. As she reflected on her marriage, she discovered that Gene wasn't the only one who was demanding of her. She discovered that she too expected herself to give regardless of how she felt. She discovered that he had learned to expect a lot from her and that she had responded in kind, in large part because of an upbringing that had firmly established this type of behavior.

Cynthia also has spent many years being a giver. She has devoted herself to meeting the needs of her husband and her family. The only person she neglected to take care of was herself. Although she is a strong woman, she failed to set limits on what she would tolerate. She failed to consider the effect her husband's behavior would have on her. Naively, she thought that if she simply continued to give, she would eventually be rewarded.

Some people say we teach people how to treat us. If we teach people to respect our boundaries, they will often do so. If we teach them that our fences are made of paper and easily pushed aside, they will not take our boundaries seriously. We are responsible for teaching others what we are willing to give and then for giving with a cheerful heart (2 Corinthians 9:7).

Repairing Damaged Boundaries

What are we to do if our boundaries are damaged? What should we do if we have struggled in a marriage with someone who has repeatedly violated our boundaries? You may feel so fragile, so violated, that you are unsure if you can ever repair the fences.

Some time ago, I worked with a 35-year-old man who was bogged down by feelings of resentment and bitterness. Jake's wife, Colleen, had begun spending evenings out with her friends while he watched their adolescent children. Feeling threatened and angry, he reacted in a hostile, controlling manner. He strongly protested against this sudden change in her behavior, but his protests only led to more absence on her part.

Jake confessed that he felt powerless to change her behavior. He told me he had demanded that she change, but this alienated them even more. She was determined to go out with her friends one or two nights a week, insisting nothing was wrong with what she was doing. As the weeks turned into months and Jake sensed the warmth and commitment of their marriage slipping away, he sought counseling.

Colleen's behavior deeply wounded Jake, and his reaction apparently wounded her. He admitted that he had been controlling, judging her behavior and putting down her friends. He could see now how these behaviors infuriated her. Each partner was guilty of violating the other's boundaries, almost to the point of ruining their marriage. Was there any hope, he wondered?

I asked Jake to tell me, as objectively as possible, what Colleen might be feeling.

"She's told me a bunch of times recently that she is just hungry for female companionship. She's told me I don't have any reason to feel threatened and that she isn't going to do anything to jeopardize our marriage. She says she works hard and needs time away from home to blow off a little steam and have some laughs with her friends. She's made it clear she hates it when I try to control. She says it only makes her angry."

I asked Jake if he could think of any examples of excessive control on his part at any time during their marriage

"I don't really think so," he said. "But Colleen would probably disagree. I suppose I haven't been a very good listener at times. I guess that's what she's looking for from her friends."

What happened to Jake and Colleen is not uncommon. One partner wants something that the other finds disturbing. One makes futile attempts to control the other's behavior. Yet so often, the more one tries to control another, the more the undesirable behavior escalates.

Jake and I considered his options. We carefully reviewed how he was responsible for his behavior alone, not his wife's. We considered Colleen's need to get away from family obligations, the house, and the kids to be with her friends. We reflected on how others often have limitations on what they are willing and able to give. Colleen certainly seemed intent on acting out her particular beliefs about her need to spend time with friends, and Jake's behavior only made matters worse. Jake felt that his boundaries were being violated—having to watch their children while she went out with friends—but he had to be careful not to violate her boundaries.

Through counseling, Jake was able to back off from his angry, controlling behavior and approach Colleen from a softer, more loving position. He was gradually able to share his feelings with her while she shared hers with him. He was able to understand that she was not betraying their marriage in any way.

They agreed to talk to their pastor and objectively seek ways to work out their differences. They were able to hammer out a solution that worked for both of them, thereby averting a disaster in their marriage.

Guard Your Heart

Jake and Colleen worked out their difficulties. He eased off his control and his criticism and began to support her desire to spend some well-deserved time with her friends. Consequently, Colleen responded to his gestures by expressing a desire to spend more time with Jake. They learned to honor one another's boundaries, respect their differences, and live in harmony. But what if you are married to someone who is not honoring your boundaries? What if he or she is continuously violating your boundaries? Drs. Townsend and Cloud, in their book *Boundaries in Marriage,* offer this warning:

> Sometimes one of the partners in a hurtful relationship is not willing to change. The partner continues to do hurtful things. Or, sometimes a spouse may have betrayed a trust or had an affair, and even though he has repented, not enough time has passed for the spouse to prove himself trustworthy. In these situations, trust may not be wise. But, it is prudent to continue to interact in the relationship and to work the problem out.[3]

Townsend and Cloud offer a number of scenarios where this counsel may apply and provide suggestions for how you might respond.

- "I love you, but I don't trust you. I can't be that close until we work this out."
- "When you can be kind, we can be close again."
- "When you show you are serious about getting some help, I will feel safe enough to open up to you again."
- "I can't share deep feelings if you are going to punish me for them."

These words may be jarring for you to hear or to share with your mate. Make no mistake—boundaries have edges to them. They may be sharp, but they define who we are, establish how we are different from others, and protect what lies within those boundaries. We have a mandate to treat our bodies and minds as temples of the Holy Spirit.

Townsend and Cloud note that the restoration process may require some physical distance between you and another person.

They tell us that distance can provide time to think, to heal, and to learn new things. Couples sometimes need to separate themselves from one another because the conversation has become too heated. In cases of emotional abuse, a separation may be essential. Or one of the partners may be faced with an addiction, and a temporary separation may be necessary for treatment.

You may need to guard your heart with some emotional or even physical distance until you feel safe moving closer. A word of caution is in order, however. We must search our hearts to ensure that our motives are pure. "Impure hearts use boundaries to act out feelings such as revenge and anger. Because none of us is pure, we have to search our motives for establishing boundaries to make sure that they serve love and not our impure motives."[4]

A Path of Love

With all of our discussion on boundaries and replacing our paper fences with more substantial barriers, we must not forget the larger law of love. Even with personal and painful violations to our boundaries (which are likely to happen when you get close to others), we must realize that love and forgiveness are crucial for any relationship. In fact, to *not* risk loving and forgiving is to lack healthy boundaries.

Consider for a moment the people who have been so wounded that they have decided never to get close to others again. When we hear Cynthia's poignant story of rejection, do we not wish for love to find her again? Do we not whisper a deep and sympathetic prayer for God to reach into her life and provide the balm of healing? When we imagine Kate's inner struggle, which involved trading security for self-esteem, do we not want to champion her to love herself?

When we talk about fences and healthy boundaries, we must remember that the fences must be strong but not inflexible. Firm, but not rigid and impenetrable. We must leave room for vulnerability to have its way. Love cannot exist without it.

The goal of establishing healthy boundaries is to share our love for others from a position of freedom. When we realize who we are and what is important to us and understand that God loves us, we are free to give ourselves to others without fear. We are free to *not* demand our way, as contradictory as that may initially seem to what we have said in this chapter. Secure in our love for God and ourselves, and sure of what is healthy for us and our mates, we are free to give more of ourselves away.

The teachers of the law approached Jesus and asked about the most important commandment. He said, "Love the Lord your God with all your heart and with all your soul and with all your mind and with all your strength. The second is this: Love your neighbor as yourself" (Mark 12:30).

Certainly this is how Jesus lived His life. He set healthy boundaries, saying no at times to bad things and yes to good things. The New Testament provides examples of Jesus saying no and pushing away from the crowds. He sought privacy to pray to the Father in Gethsemane. He gave the disciples authority to drive out evil spirits and then gave them clear instructions for entering a home. "If the home is deserving, let your peace rest on it; if it is not, let your peace return to you. If anyone will not welcome you or listen to your words, shake the dust off your feet when you leave that home or town" (Matthew 10:13-14).

Jesus was just as comfortable saying yes to situations and events. A leper came to Jesus and asked if He was willing to make him clean. "I am willing," Jesus said (Matthew 8:3). He was willing to go and heal the centurion's son. He makes an unusual request of the Samaritan woman by asking her for a drink of water. He chose to eat with tax collectors, harlots, and the disenfranchised in spite of criticism from the teachers of the law. Repeatedly, we see Jesus as someone who is perfectly comfortable in His own skin. He is able to say yes and no.

But in freedom, Jesus chose to deny Himself and serve others, expecting nothing in return. He was in perfect control of Himself and thus was free to deny His own needs at times in the larger pursuit of love. Of course, Jesus made the ultimate sacrifice of His safety and well-being so that He could offer us the gift of eternal life. He paid the ultimate price, sacrificing Himself in order to provide us with life and love. What better example for us to follow!

How much do you give in your marriage? How much do you strive to meet your spouse's needs? Do you have resentments that need healing? An honest response to these questions can set you on the higher path of unconditional love.

Chapter Nine

Stop Using That Untamed Tongue:
Put Away Angry Words

If the word has the potency to revive and make us free,
it also has the power to blind, imprison, and destroy.
—RALPH ELLISON

The Iroquois Theater Disaster of 1903, the worst fire Chicago has known, was the tragedy that should never have happened. In this blight on the city's history, more than six hundred people died. Charred bodies were piled high behind the unnecessarily locked doors of a theater because the management did not follow fire policies or have practical emergency guidelines in place.

Author Anthony Hatch, in his book *Tinderbox: The Iroquois Disaster of 1903,* notes that this theater was the safest playhouse in America at the turn of the twentieth century and rivaled anything in Europe. Apparently officials looked the other way when an over-capacity crowd packed the theater that Christmas week more than a hundred years ago. A short circuit in a backstage spotlight resulted in the worst tragedy in American theater history. In less than 20 minutes more than 600 people, mostly women and children, perished in the quick-spreading fire. Would-be rescuers had no time to react—to save the helpless victims from the horrific inferno.

An account of the calamity suggests that the crowd rushed to the exits like a flood of water trying to force its way through small openings—and these openings were blocked. Victims were piled ten high behind the locked doors. They had no way of escape. What people thought was considered the safest theater was now a tinderbox—ready to go up in destructive flames with a single spark.

A fire is especially dreadful—the panic, asphyxiation, and maimed bodies. Even those who survive are often disfigured. Yet if we are to limit disasters—regardless of the type—we must learn from examples such as this.

Like the circuit breaker that malfunctioned in the Iroquois Theater disaster, the tongue—when used in an angry way—has the capacity to create sparks that can set a marriage ablaze. A relationship can be damaged in moments by the fiery attack of the tongue. And in the tinderbox of a dried relationship, a spark can completely raze the bond between husband and wife.

So here is our next critical mistake—using the sharp tongue in an untamed, angry way. Like fire, it is a killer. It destroys people, relationships, and marriages.

A Tinderbox

The tinderbox was an early invention in the history of fire. It was most commonly a container with flint, steel, and dry shavings of straw or hemp used to start fires. It fell out of usage with the invention of matches.

The image is clear. Just as Anthony Hatch likened the theater to a tinderbox, we can picture marriages in a similar light. Just as we often consider ourselves invulnerable to the ravages of fire in our homes, we also want to believe that the ravages of the tongue cannot set our marriages ablaze. That simply is not true.

The apostle James likened the tongue to a spark in a tinderbox. Consider what he says about the tongue and angry words:

> Likewise the tongue is a small part of the body, but it makes great boasts. Consider what a great forest is set on fire by a small spark. The tongue is also a fire, a world of evil among the parts of the body. It corrupts the whole person, sets the whole course of his life on fire, and is itself set on fire by hell (James 3:5-6).

James uses powerful imagery here. He says the tongue is a fire—not that it is *like* a fire, but that it *is* a fire. He goes on to call it a "world of evil." This powerful, potent language forces us to pause and consider what he is saying. The tongue is a fire? The tongue is a world of evil? Surely, he is prone to hyperbole.

I don't think so.

James catches our attention by likening the tongue—and our speech—to a fire that is out of control. He says the source of the tongue's wickedness is hell itself, that Satan can use the tongue to divide people and pit them against one another. We may deny this, but personal experience tells us his words are true. We have seen first-hand the damage the tongue can do. We have seen how quickly the wrong words can spread destruction like the fire in the theater, like a spark setting a forest ablaze.

We know James' words are true.

Playing with Fire

Fire is one of those elements that is either our friend, keeping us warm and dry, or our foe, creating incomparable damage. Likewise, the tongue can either encourage or destroy. As James said, "With the tongue we praise our Lord and Father, and with it we curse men, who have been made in God's likeness" (James 3:9).

Fire creates searing heat. But perhaps most destructively, fire consumes the oxygen we need to survive, causing asphyxiation. Fire robs us of life just as the tongue sets a mortal blaze in our marriages, stealing their life.

For any fire to continue, however, it needs fuel. I received a vivid lesson about fire and fuel one warm summer day when I was about ten years old. I was lying in the tall grass behind my house with a couple of buddies. With stalks of dried grass hanging out of our mouths we were telling stories and enjoying ourselves. Life couldn't have been sweeter.

To ten-year-olds, those stalks of grass were temptingly similar to the forbidden cigarette, and one of us wondered what it would be like to "smoke" a few of those blades of grass. It all seemed innocent enough. We gathered our "cigarettes" and proceeded to light up. Suddenly, without warning, a spark caught in a bundle of dried grass, and then another, until we were faced with an inferno beyond our control. Realizing the potential danger of the fire, we ran for my dad. Three screaming boys immediately caught his attention. We formed a "bucket brigade" and were able to douse the fire and get on to the next important issue—explaining all of this to my very angry father. I don't know what scared us more, the raging fire or the sparks coming from my dad!

As you might imagine, "I'm sorry" did not satisfy my enraged father. He had scolded us before for other irresponsible antics, and this day's misbehavior would result in me being grounded for weeks. We had to apologize to the entire fire department crew and listen to the longest lecture imaginable on fire safety from the chief.

A marriage can be tinder dry at times, ready for a spark to ignite things. A season of dryness, or ongoing conflict, can set the stage for an angry outburst of deadly proportions.

If we are to protect marriages from the unruly tongue and its accompanying fire, we must maintain careful watch on both the tongue and the fuel that feeds the fire.

Fuel for the Fire

Karen and Douglas came to see me because they were having "communication problems" in their marriage. Married only six years, they were already considering divorce. Karen was an attractive, spirited, 26-year-old woman who worked at a local bank. Her husband, Douglas, also 26, was a husky, reserved man, dressed in a suit. He worked as a mortgage broker and conveyed a firm demeanor. He offered little humor during our first meeting.

Both Karen and Douglas were college-educated and had sophisticated verbal skills. They had clearly honed these skills on one another, using them like swords in a duel. Their testy banter began from the onset of our counseling.

Karen chose to sit in a chair as far from Douglas as possible. Douglas glared at Karen.

I asked them what had brought them to counseling.

"We can't seem to agree on anything," Karen said sharply. "I want Douglas to help me out more at home with our two young kids, and he feels that he already does enough. He says it's not his job."

"Yeah, right" Douglas said sarcastically. "I said that I would be willing to do more housework if you'd help me out with some of the chores outside the house. I just want things to be equal."

Both eyed one another as if appraising an enemy before battle.

"I don't think that's the issue at all," Karen said. "I think you're lazy and just don't want to help out with the housework. Your dad never does a thing for your mom, and you expect me to wait on you the same way. I'm sick of it. You think it's enough to go to the office and then come home late and play with the kids for a few minutes. Even my friends think you do too little to help out. Besides, I keep my car clean and lubed. I don't get any help from you there."

Douglas snickered disparagingly at Karen's words.

"It's a pretty big stretch to call me lazy, given that I work sixty hours a week and bring home seventy-five percent of our income. I wouldn't call that lazy. You're the one who has it easy. You're the one who seems to have extra time to spend with your friends, talking about everyone under the sun. Forty hours a week and keeping the house up? That doesn't sound too tough to me."

The tension was already so thick in the room that you could cut it with a knife. I wondered what had happened to create such hostility between these people. I also wondered how they talked to one another in the confines of their home if they were willing to be so brutal with one another in the presence of a stranger.

"Folks, I want to shift gears with you for a few moments. I sense a lot of anger, and you are making a lot of verbal attacks on one another. With your permission, I'd like to take a history of your relationship. Specifically, I want to look at when you started talking to each other the way you're talking today."

Reluctantly, they agreed to spend some time discussing the history of their marriage. We discovered that they were careless in how they talked to one another from the early stages of their marriage. They were accustomed to aggressively sharing their feelings when annoyed with one another. Even as they shared their history, they were tempted to say something biting to their partner at every pause in the conversation. They lived in a tinderbox, with all the elements necessary to fuel the most destructive marital fires.

See if any of these "fuels for the fire" exist in your relationship.

First, *when people attack one another, they are usually feeling hurt themselves.* This was certainly true for Karen and Douglas. Each admitted to feeling wounded by the other's words and attacked in retaliation. Healing would occur only when they could acknowledge their own wounds and find other ways of expressing their pain.

Anger is a secondary emotion. Consider exploring your marriage to see if your anger may be an easy cover-up for one or more of the emotions in this group. Together, they are known as GIFT:

- *Guilt*—anger often covers feelings of unexpressed guilt. Karen may have been feeling guilty about not providing more parental time for her children.

- *Inferiority*—anger often covers feelings of insecurity or inferiority. Douglas may have felt that he was not as effective a parent as he should have been, and Karen's attacks threatened his fragile self-esteem.

- *Fear*—this is often an emotion that is difficult to express. Both Karen and Douglas may have been feeling frightened about their marriage being so out of control.

- *Trauma*—conflicts may reawaken previous trauma in your life, creating hypersensitivity to an issue. This issue may have intensified in Karen and Douglas' relationship because of earlier conflicts in their families of origin.

Second, *partners may feel unappreciated in the marriage.* Douglas and Karen revealed how their busyness and their desire to advance in their professions had taken a toll on their relationship. They were spending far less time appreciating one another than they had in the early stages of their courtship and marriage. They revealed that their lives now consisted of taking care of the details of managing their home and family. Too often, they left no time for each other. They rarely made room for that special night out or even a quiet conversation. Most evenings, they simply skimmed a few pages of the newspaper before falling into bed and turning out the light.

Third, *couples often bottle up their pain.* Karen and Douglas had not found a way to talk openly and effectively about their frustrations. Thus, they drove anger and resentment underground. They buried their hurt only to have it resurface in problems that were not the real issue.

Finally, *talking to one another with a sharp tongue becomes commonplace.* Without a critical level of awareness, untamed sarcasm can creep into a marriage and become part of every conversation. Karen justified talking to Douglas this way because of the hurt she was experiencing and because he talked to her in this manner—and vice versa. They had become somewhat desensitized to the critical, angry language they were delivering.

Karen and Douglas had big problems. The problems they mentioned were not overwhelming, but the way they talked to one another had set a blaze in their marriage.

Resolving role issues in a marriage is not an overpowering problem. But when marriage partners hurt each other's feelings and do not address issues effectively, they create fuel for the fire. And the fire in their marriage had left little oxygen. Their relationship was suffocating.

Subsequently, they were contemplating ending their marriage to get the breathing room they desperately needed. Leaving the marriage, however, would not end their pain. They would simply transport their destructive communication habits into their next relationships.

The Untamed Tongue

We can easily criticize Karen and Douglas for using their untamed tongues as weapons. They may rationalize their reasons for directing verbal missiles at each other, but the attacks only serve to damage the integrity of their marriage. The vocal grenades do absolutely nothing to heal their broken relationship or to provide answers to their disagreements.

Clifton Fadiman, in *The Little, Brown Book of Anecdotes,* shares the story of Abraham Lincoln's secretary of war, Edwin Stanton, who apparently had some trouble with a prominent general who accused him, in insulting terms, of favoritism. Stanton complained to President Lincoln, who suggested that he write the general a sharp letter. Stanton did so and showed the strongly worded missive to Lincoln, who applauded his powerful language.

"What are you going to do with it?" he asked.

Stanton was surprised. "Send it," he said.

Lincoln shook his head. He suggested that sending the letter would be ill-advised.

"You don't want to send that letter," he said. "Put it in the stove. That's what I do when I have written a letter while I am angry. It's a good letter and you had a good time writing it and feel better. Now, burn it, and write another."[1]

Who among us has not felt like Stanton after suffering emotional injury? We want to spew out our feelings, unedited, to rid ourselves of the venom we are holding within. We want to attack. We want others to hurt the way we are hurting. Yet as Lincoln wisely says, that is not the best course of action. It only causes more problems in the long run. It unleashes a flame in dry grass, causing a conflagration we may not easily contain.

The Scriptures are rife with examples of problems stemming from the untamed tongue. Much of the gospel story is set in the context of relationships, so we should not be surprised at how much counsel the Bible gives us about the way we talk to one another. Consider these important admonitions about our speech:

- "For since there is jealousy and quarreling among you, are you not worldly?" (1 Corinthians 3:3).

- "Make every effort to keep the unity of the spirit through the bond of peace" (Ephesians 4:3).

≈ "But now you must rid yourselves of all such things as these: anger, rage, malice, slander, and filthy language from your lips" (Colossians 3:8).

Let's consider a few more examples of the untamed tongue.

Gossip

We know better than to gossip about others, yet we seem to have an insatiable need to do so anyway. Gather around any office water cooler and you're likely to get an earful about someone else's problems.

I recently caught myself talking about another person in a dishonorable way. A colleague had acted in an unprofessional manner toward me, so I felt justified in criticizing her. Because I was insecure and a bit frightened, I covered my pain with feelings of righteous indignation. I fueled my anger with words that demeaned her character. Another colleague was my audience, and for a moment nothing seemed wrong with my actions. But even as I was gossiping, the Holy Spirit whispered to me that I would gain nothing by inflating myself and humiliating her. I felt ashamed of my actions.

Putting Others Down

When I feel injured or insecure, I am quick to want to put down my assailant. Although the more mature part of me says, *Don't do it,* the immature, wounded part says, *Go after him. Hit him where it hurts.* At these moments I try to honor my hurt but reconsider my temptation to hurt others in return. I remind myself that what I really want is not dissension in relationships but rather peace.

As you engage others in conversation, you might notice what I have noticed: We seem to have a huge need to put people down. Being critical of the motives and behaviors of others is easy. We all seem very quick to judge the motives of friends, family members, spouses, coworkers, and strangers without fully giving them a chance. But if we truly understand others, we will have little need to put them down because we will realize why they do what they do.

The apostle James has more valuable words for us, this time about quarreling. He reminds us that our attacks on others often have no legitimate cause.

James asks, "What causes fights and quarrels among you? Don't they come from the desires that battle within you? You want something but don't get it. You kill and covet, but you cannot have what you want. You quarrel and fight" (James 4:1).

Ouch.

James' words hit us hard. He says that the quarrels do not come from without—as the result of other people acting poorly toward us—but from within, as a result of our own battling desires.

I want to rail against his words. "But James," I'd like to say, "you don't know this colleague I was complaining about earlier. How can you say the quarrel comes from my motives, my desire to have something I do not have? You don't know what she did to me. You're being unfair."

As if by a law of human nature, we feel compelled to twist the truth to make ourselves look better. We also want to manipulate things so we have the highest likelihood of getting what we want.

Bragging

The Scriptures caution us about bragging. The apostle Paul says, "For by the grace given me I say to every one of you: Do not think of yourself more highly than you ought, but rather think of yourself with sober judgment, in accordance with the measure of faith God has given you" (Romans 12:3).

As I listened to Karen and Douglas, I was astounded by the pomposity that crowded the room. You could almost see the rarified air that encircled them. Noses turned up, heads cocked slightly to the side, facial gestures magnifying their importance.

Of course, I am being sarcastic. I am chiding Karen and Douglas, and myself too, at how seriously we take ourselves. How easily we shift into this arrogant mentality! You could almost hear Karen's and Douglas's thoughts:

- ✎ I know precisely what is going on here.
- ✎ I know how to resolve this issue.
- ✎ I'm right and you're wrong.
- ✎ I have done nothing worthy of criticism.

As I shared in a previous chapter ("Stop Playing God"), this kind of attitude inevitably creates division. It fosters a "me versus you" mentality. This mind-set is not conducive to solving problems. It simply sets the stage for the untamed tongue to do its work.

False Reporting

False reporting is very common. It is not so much outright lying as it is putting a spin on things to put ourselves in a more favorable light.

During our recent national elections, I listened to talk radio. I was intrigued by the way both liberal and conservative hosts put a biased negative spin on everything about their opponents. Backers of Senator Kerry accused President Bush of entering Iraq only to advance his political agenda, making the most of the war to help him win reelection. Backers of President Bush accused Senator Kerry of being a traitor, ill-equipped and unworthy to lead our country in a time of war. Both positions were exaggerated and manipulative.

This is similar to the concept of *polarization* that I talked about earlier in the book. When angry with our mates, we are tempted to take what they are saying and put a spin on it to give ourselves an advantage. We sound like the candidate or spin-doctor who is trying to discredit the other side.

We are tempted to put spins on issues in marriage, perhaps by emphasizing what our mates do without recognizing our own foibles. Or perhaps we fail to provide the context in which our mates do something, thereby making their actions look worse than they actually are.

Exaggerating

Exaggeration is like false reporting. Here the culprits take a kernel of truth and exaggerate it for their own advantage.

Let's consider how Karen and Douglas used this technique. To hear Karen talk, you'd think that Douglas didn't do a thing around the house to help the family. To hear Douglas, you'd think that Karen had a life of leisure. Of course, both points of view are exaggerations of the truth.

What makes exaggeration even more deadly in a marriage is the impact it has on the other person. When someone exaggerates a wrongdoing, the other person usually becomes defensive. Trust is broken and the relational bridge is damaged. That bridge must be repaired before intimacy can be restored.

Complaining

Those who complain often believe that they are the ones getting a raw deal, that all the cards are stacked against them. In this version of the untamed tongue, we see the complainer playing the role of victim.

Recently, an angry 40-year-old man came to see me. He complained of unhappiness in his marriage and wondered whether he should continue with what seemed to be a hopeless situation or end his marriage. He stated that his wife of 20 years had quit showing him affection. He complained bitterly about her lack of affection in the bedroom. According to him, she worked hard at her job, took care of their three children, and effectively managed their home, but she offered no outward signs of affection unless he complained loudly enough about it. And then she was a reluctant participant.

When I asked him about his part in all of this, he became puzzled. He denied doing anything that might make her push him away. In fact, he said that he was practically the model husband. He came home promptly after work, offered to help cook and clean, and helped with their children. He had no idea how he might be contributing to this problem.

Although our friend may truly be the victim of unfortunate circumstances, my experience tells me that he is missing a critical piece of the puzzle. I suspect his wife has another version to the story, and our friend is not as helpful or encouraging as he presents. I encouraged him to go back to his wife to find out what he was like to live with and what he might do to increase the affection level in their relationship. If he is sincere in his efforts, I expect positive results.

Lying

Perhaps nothing is as destructive to a marriage as dishonesty. Lying can punch gaping holes in a relationship. Those holes are exceptionally difficult to heal.

We can be dishonest about trivial things—the amount of money we spent on our last purchase—or large things—where we spent the night when we didn't come home. Any kind of dishonesty will add to the acrimony in your marriage.

Betrayed trust is difficult to restore. When major instances of dishonesty have occurred—such as infidelity in your marriage—these breeches usually require professional help to heal.

Why is dishonesty such a huge issue? Because it erodes the foundation of safety we must have if we are to risk getting close to someone. If we cannot trust our mate, we are unlikely to risk making our deepest selves vulnerable. A healthy marriage requires trust and safety to thrive.

Taming the Tongue

You can use the tongue both for cursing and blessing, and fortunately, you can choose to tame the tongue and use it to bless your mate. The decision is yours.

What would happen in your marriage if you decided to put away anger, complaining, criticizing, and manipulating? What if you decided to make Ephesians 4:29 your goal? "Do not let any unwholesome [untamed] talk come out of your mouths, but only what is helpful for building others up according to their needs, that it may benefit those who listen."

Whoa! No unwholesome talk. Only talk that edifies others. Talk that will meet their needs at the time.

For beneficial conversation, you need to be tuned in to your spouse's needs. You can begin by praying for strength to set aside your hurt and allowing God to "strengthen you with power through his Spirit in your inner being" (Ephesians 3:16). If we have done our homework, we have spent time really listening to our mates so that we are aware of what they need:

- a word of encouragement
- a word of challenge
- a word of sympathy
- a word of empathy
- a word of concern

Offering a word according to your spouse's need will create true intimacy. This kind of communication will surprise you with its incredible benefits.

Antidote to Contempt

You may wonder, *But what if our marriage is too full of contempt and anger to do this?* John Gottman has written extensively on issues pertaining to the untamed tongue. In his book *The Seven Principles for Making Marriage Work,* he talks about anger, which he considers to be a killer of marriages, and he offers the potential cure.

Gottman believes that if your relationship is marred by a lack of mutual fondness and admiration, it is in trouble. Contempt—which is one common associate of the biting, untamed tongue—signals that fondness and admiration have dissipated. But Gottman reminds us that hope is still alive. He suggests the following antidote: "By simply reminding yourself of your spouse's positive qualities—even as you grapple with each other's flaws—you can prevent a happy marriage from deteriorating. The simple reason is that fondness and admiration are antidotes to contempt."[2]

Through counseling, Karen and Douglas became aware of the damage their angry words could cause. Though their anger took time to dissipate, they learned the art of "conflict containment"—putting their angry words aside while affirming the strengths and attributes that had originally drawn them to each other. Before long, they found the mood in their marriage beginning to shift, something I have seen happen many times.

Once their anger had dissipated and they had agreed that volatile words had no place in their marriage, their moods lightened. They were now prepared to begin treating each other with kindness and respect. They discovered that they still really cared for one another, and they began planning a series of special outings to celebrate their new relationship. They vowed never to speak to one another in a derogatory way again. Karen and Douglas demonstrated that when couples "plant seeds and pull weeds," they can expect a rich harvest in their relationship.

Cleaning the Slate

When emotional debris has cluttered your marriage and your untamed tongues have waged war on each other, perhaps you need to clean the slate. Cleaning the slate can begin with what I call "do overs." Hit with an epiphany of self-awareness in the middle of a knockdown, drag-out fight, I will say, "This isn't going very well. How 'bout we start over again?"

With a bit of practice, your mate can also learn to sense impending verbal destruction and willingly call a halt to the conflict. Then you start the conversation over again, this time from a better perspective.

Perhaps you are in a marriage where feelings are hurt and damaging words flow with too much regularity. You may need to "clean the slate" with a broader brush stroke. This means sitting down with your mate and agreeing to let the past go, to stop holding grudges, and to start over.

Yes, we have the right to hold onto our ill will. But we all know that will get us nowhere.

Drs. Les and Leslie Parrott, in their book *When Bad Things Happen to Good Marriages,* remind us of what we already know but need to hear again. "The failure to give or receive forgiveness probably accounts for nearly every marriage that does not endure...Carrying rage against our partner does more harm to us than to them."[3]

As hard as it is to forgive, we must do it if we want a healthy marriage. If we don't deal with the resentment deep inside, we are likely to unleash verbal venom at any moment.

Blessed Are the Poor in Spirit

Taming the tongue includes biting that tongue in critical moments and allowing God to perform surgery on the heart as well. In fact, Jesus talks as much about the condition of the heart as He does about our actions. Both need our attention, but real outward change requires a changed heart.

If we want to experience significant change in our hearts, the best place to turn for instruction is the Sermon on the Mount. Jesus' longest discourse is full of valuable advice on this subject.

Consider the first Be-Attitude in our pursuit of the tamed tongue. What would happen to our speech in marriage if we were to pursue, wholeheartedly, being poor in spirit? As the first Be-Attitude says, "Blessed are the poor in spirit, for theirs is the kingdom of heaven" (Matthew 5:3). What does Jesus mean when He calls us to be "poor in spirit"? Emmett Fox, in his classic, *The Sermon on the Mount*, says this:

> To be poor in spirit means to have emptied yourself of all desire to exercise personal self-will, and, what is just as important, to have renounced all preconceived opinions in the whole-hearted search for God. It means to be willing to set aside your present habits of thought, your way of life if necessary; to jettison, in fact, anything and everything that can stand in the way of your finding God.[4]

The third Be-Attitude is also extremely helpful to us as we pursue a tamed tongue. "Blessed are the meek, for they will inherit the earth" (Matthew 5:5). This passage speaks to our thirst for power, which is one of the culprits most likely to wield the vengeance of the untamed tongue. The desire to have our way, to make our point, to make certain things happen to our liking, is a root cause of the sharp, untamed tongue. Those who seek meekness will discover the difference between asserting their opinions—at the right times and for the right motives—and asserting their will for the sake of personal power.

Perhaps the Be-Attitude offering the greatest cure for taming the tongue is the one that offers just the opposite of rage—peace. "Blessed are the peacemakers, for they will be called sons of God" (Matthew 5:9). Consistent with the Gospel message and many of the apostle Paul's writings, peace is surely one of the hallmarks of Christianity. It is also one of the most wonderful fruits of the Spirit. But peace cannot coexist with the untamed tongue.

As you listen to others on your walk through the world, I challenge you to pay attention to people's speech—both their words and their tone. I suspect you will find, as I do, that much speech serves only to produce conflict and chaos. In marriage, speech is often responsible for creating distance and hard feelings. Far too rarely do I hear soft words, kind words, encouraging words. Yet that is precisely what the Sermon on the Mount asks from us.

There they are. The golden truths that will set us free from bondage to self-will, self-adulation, self-aggrandizement. If, by the power of the Holy Spirit, we can free ourselves from the stranglehold of the almighty ego, perhaps we really can tame the tongue. Perhaps then, with a softer spirit, we can learn that giving is better than receiving and that loving others is far more gratifying than having our own way.

Jesus, of course, is our preeminent example of selflessness. In one of the most incredible passages of Scripture, we learn of how Jesus prepared to empty Himself. We read in the letter to the Philippians that He "made himself nothing, taking the very nature of a servant, being made in human likeness...and became obedient to death" (Philippians 2:7-8).

I remember learning a song as a child that still brings tears to my eyes. The song said, in essence, that Jesus walked freely to the cross—

beaten, scourged, and ridiculed—when He could have called ten thousand angels to set Him free. He could have waved His arms and, in an instant, called forth a hundred thousand troops to bind His captors and complete His triumph. He could have spat upon them and laughed at their shameful actions.

But He didn't.

He wouldn't.

Perhaps because of who He was, He couldn't. It was not in His heart to act the way we act so often.

In some small way, we must understand that poverty of spirit is the way of Jesus. It is the only real method for taming the tongue. Make no mistake: This is not optional if you wish to have a healthy marriage or a healthy relationship of any kind.

If you practice the principles in this chapter, including seeking a spirit of humility, you will reap great rewards in your marriage. And you will inherit the kingdom of heaven as well!

Chapter Ten

Stop Being Distant:
Dare to Come Close

A loving heart is the truest wisdom.
—CHARLES DICKENS

Traveling into the metropolitan city of Seattle is an incredible challenge. On a recent trip I had hoped to avoid the crush of traffic by leaving a little early. No such luck. The mob of people is inescapable.

As I painstakingly maneuvered through the endless trail of cars, practicing deep breathing to stay calm, I reflected on the congestion. Numerous lanes were packed with cars; people were generally riding alone, migrating like frenzied elk from one grazing area to another.

I imagined the hours these urbanites spent commuting each year, practically touching each other yet never exchanging a word. I imagined some sitting in silence while others blasted music through their craniums.

Anxious for an opportunity to increase my snail-like pace, I peered enviously over at the car pool lane, peppered with just a handful of cars. No buses in sight. I wondered why folks were so intent on riding alone instead of carpooling. I wondered why more people didn't use mass transit. Busy people, sharing the same experience, were miles apart.

Glancing to either side of the interstate, I saw rows of housing developments crowded together. Some were obviously well established. Others seemed to have sprung up since my last visit.

I am not a fan of housing developments. When I first lived in them, I imagined they would be the perfect way to create a sense of community while maintaining individuality. But that was not the case at all. In fact, in one housing complex where my family lived, we did not know the first names of the neighbors on either side of us. I waved to them every day of the year yet never took the time to get to know them. Good intentions never got the job done. Even living in such close proximity, we were virtually isolated from one another.

Freeways and housing developments illustrate how we struggle with attachment and intimacy. People in our society have a growing sense of our distance from one another. We know that we are on the brink of a serious problem with isolation and loneliness. We are becoming more aware that we are moving through life at a breakneck pace, slowed only by our occasional stop at the neighborhood Starbucks for our daily dose of caffeine and community.

As I gripped the steering wheel of my car, driving alone amidst the press of other cars, I remembered that this societal problem is also a deeply personal one for many people.

And I recalled a recent telephone conversation I had with a woman named Trudy.

Distance

In a fairly typical broadcast, a promotional effort for my most recent book, *Does Your Man Have the Blues?* I was talking to the radio host in Kansas City from my home about how depressed men isolate themselves as part of their blues. Although the focus was on men, we also discussed how male depression affects wives.

Trudy was brave. She dared to call in and share her pain. In a few short minutes we learned a great deal about her. Perhaps in the anonymity of radio she felt free to allow us a glimpse of her life.

"My husband and I live separate lives," she said. "I feel lost, numb. We eat dinner in front of the television because we don't know what to say to each other. When dinner is over he goes to his den to work. I watch another TV program. I hear him heading for bed without saying goodnight. I'm afraid to go to bed with him because he might want to be intimate, and I can't think about that right now in our relationship. We still go to church together, but I have no idea of what he thinks about God. We don't share anything spiritual either. I don't feel close to him at all, physically or emotionally."

"How long have things been like this, Trudy?" I asked.

"Years. We don't fight. We don't share anything emotional. We don't really talk—not in depth anyway—and I'm starving for that."

"Have you told him that you want things to be better?"

"Yes. But when I tell him we have to make changes, he just says, 'I don't know what to do.' The problem is that I don't know what to do either."

"You sound very lonely, Trudy."

"I'm dying of loneliness. It's amazing that we can spend so much time together and still be like total strangers. I wonder what's wrong with us."

There was a brief silence. I felt sadness for Trudy. I could hear and feel her pain. I wondered how many other listeners were strangers to their own spouses. How many couples lived empty, lonely lives like Trudy's? How many felt helpless to make changes that might invigorate their marriages?

"Trudy, I have bad news and good news. First, the bad news. You sound like many others I counsel who have forgotten how important it is to nourish their marriages. They have slowly and subtly let things go, thinking the relationship would simply survive on its own. But too often, they find that is not the case."

I let the words sink in. I visualized a woman, clutching the receiver of her phone, frightened to verbalize her terrible truth—and our next critical mistake—*being distant in marriage.*

"Now, are you ready for some good news?" I said brightly.

"Absolutely," she said through her tears. "We need help."

"Yes, you do, Trudy. And help is available. I suspect your husband is feeling just as lonely and afraid as you. Like you, he doesn't know what to do to bring back the zest in your marriage. But I'll bet he would follow your lead if you gave him some ideas. The good news is that marriages can be reinvigorated. You can give a stale relationship new life. Hope is definitely available for your situation. But first I need to know if you will you agree to get into counseling to explore ideas for bringing the joy back?"

"Yes," she said.

"We're going to give you some phone numbers that you can call to receive help. Keep hoping, Trudy. Don't give up."

Even after taking other calls, I couldn't quit thinking about Trudy and her husband. I couldn't shake my own sadness for her. She had touched a chord in me, and for days I reflected on our conversation.

Like Trudy, I have let distance creep into too many important relationships. As a result, I have had to face painful truths and take ameliorative action. I have found that facing the truth about a distant relationship is the first step. I take time to consider what the relationship means to me and exactly what I am missing. I consider how I have let closeness slip away, and I determine a plan for reinvigorating the relationship. Sometimes starting the process only takes a few simple steps, such as taking the initiative to have lunch together.

Anatomy of Detachment

Trudy shared her personal story like hundreds of others I have listened to over the years in my professional practice. Like Trudy and her husband, many couples walk through life in a daze. They go to work, raise kids, coach their children's soccer teams, sing in the choir at church, come home and watch a little television, drift apart, and divorce.

We weep for those couples that do not make it. We also rail at them for not having more staying power. We may be critical of them, but we are also hypocritical—secretly aware that our own marriages are often not in much better shape.

Of course couples should never drift apart. But they do—sometimes we do too. And it happens for understandable and preventable reasons. And that is the focus of our last critical mistake—*being distant with one another.*

Let's take a closer look at Trudy's life and at what is happening in many marriages. Let's consider what she shared in those few minutes on the phone, words that are sadly echoed in thousands of homes today. Let's examine the anatomy of the emotionally separated couple. How did they get that way? What happens to reinforce the pattern?

First, *relationships are always in a gradual state of deterioration.* Although some may disagree with this statement, I believe it to be true. Like other objects that must obey the law of entropy, relationships begin to decay almost as soon as the honeymoon ends. After the wedding bells go silent and the wrapping paper from the gifts goes out with the trash, the practicalities of living can easily preoccupy us. Trudy revealed that her marriage had been gradually losing its spark. She and her husband failed to be vigilant and determined in keeping their relationship fresh.

Second, *we have an ongoing need for relationship.* Think about it. Trudy was lonely, as are many others. She wanted *real* contact. She wanted someone to listen to her, appreciate her, and understand her. These are not unreasonable requests. In fact, if individuals cannot find these ingredients in their marriages, they will look elsewhere for them. But if husbands and wives realize that their mission is to supply these needs, they need not look elsewhere.

Third, *we have a need for friendship.* Consider what you look for in a friend. Most of us want someone who will laugh with us, share stories with us, listen to our foibles, and help us look at life in new ways. Although friendship can be a challenge, it *can* be part of our marriages. Sadly, Trudy had lost this friendship with her husband. But with effort, dedication, and focus, mates can become companions again. They can remember what they enjoyed before and start doing those things again. All of us can create a new list of fun things to do with our spouses.

One couple I know has a "surprise outings" jar. Both people are responsible for putting slips of paper with interesting outings in the jar. They take turns each weekend taking one new slip out of the jar, and they do something fun together. Sometimes the outings are "tried and true" activities they have both enjoyed in the past. Sometimes they are experiences they always wanted to do but just never got around to doing. In the past month they have taken a tour of the battleship in the Bremerton harbor, taken a trip to the Seattle zoo, and spent an afternoon having lunch and browsing magazines and books together in a local bookstore.

Fourth, *friends are interesting people to be with.* Trudy said that being with her husband had become boring, perhaps because they had both so lost interest in the other that they preferred being apart. Vibrant marriages are made up of partners who recognize the importance of being vital and energetic. They rigorously guard against dullness in their marriages.

Finally, *we have a need for intimacy.* I have described intimacy as *into-me-see.* But achieving this level of closeness is far easier said than done. It requires all of the above ingredients and more. It requires a dedication to being transparent with your partner. It requires vigorous attention to creating safety in your relationship so that both of you are willing to be open with each other. When that happens, joy and intimacy will follow.

Desire for Intimacy

If I have learned one thing in more than 28 years of working with people, it is this: We all have a deep and abiding need to belong, to be loved, and to be understood. It is that simple and that profound. You can find a million ways to say it, sing it, or write it, but the message is the same—we have an innate desire for intimacy. Every disruption of a marital relationship has at its root some disorder in healthy intimacy.

But what exactly is intimacy? We hear the word so often that its meaning becomes a little fuzzy. Janet Woititz, author of *Struggle for Intimacy,* offers a few ways to think about it. She suggests that intimacy can grow when these things are true:

- I can be me.
- You can be you.
- We can be us.
- I can grow.
- You can grow.
- We can grow together.

She adds this definition of intimacy: "Intimacy means that you have a love relationship with another person where you offer, and you are offered, validation, understanding, and a sense of being valued intellectually, emotionally, and physically."[1]

As I considered her definition, I found myself saying yes to it because it made sense. I want to be in relationships where I can truly be me. This is harder than it first sounds. I want to be able to have opinions that may be different from yours, and I want to feel free to share them without shame. I want to be in relationships where I value other people and give them freedom to disagree with me, perhaps even to the point of encouraging our differences. And I want us to be able to grow together.

When I am in a relationship where any of those vital components are missing, I withdraw. Perhaps not physically. I may look like I am still involved. But I create a protective membrane around myself so that you cannot fully see into me. If I do not feel safe to share my feelings and beliefs, I will not be sticking around.

Flesh of My Flesh

Why do you suppose we ache so badly when an intimate relationship is broken, even temporarily? Why do we feel as if we were literally disintegrating, our flesh tearing apart, when a marriage disintegrates? Why can't we simply wipe the dust off our feet and move on to greener pastures? I think the answer to those questions is in the Genesis story of creation—in the very heart of God Himself.

Our innate desire for intimacy comes, of course, from our Creator. It is no accident that we have a desire—some may call it a need—to draw close to one another and to God. We have been created for relationship. Jesus was an example to us of the Word becoming flesh. He taught us the gospel in the context of relationships. Intimacy with our mate was part of God's design.

We must remind ourselves that woman was not formed of new elements. She was not taken from dust, nor was she separate from man. She was taken from Adam, a part of him, to become his bride. Adam's first words were, "This is now bone of my bones and flesh of my flesh; she shall be called 'woman,' for she was taken out of man"

(Genesis 2:23). In her book *Fashioned for Intimacy,* Jane Hansen makes this observation:

> Adam obviously recognized something of himself in her. She was bone of his bones and flesh of his flesh. He welcomed and received her, claiming her as part of himself...There was an awareness that God had made them for each other, that he had specifically fashioned this union and there would be an interdependency between them. Although they were two separate beings having very different qualities, their destiny was to be together.[2]

After creating man and woman, God further makes His intentions clear. "For this reason (because they are bone of bone and flesh of flesh) a man will leave his father and mother and be united to his wife, and they will become one flesh" (Genesis 2:24). Hansen shares another insight about the power of this passage:

> This directive from God is recorded four times in Scripture. It was first voiced here in Genesis 2, repeated by Jesus as recorded in Matthew 19 and Mark 10, and repeated by Paul in Ephesians 5. When a word is mentioned once in the Bible, we need to take a special note. When it is mentioned four times, it becomes a red-flag alert! God is wanting us to pay very close attention.[3]

We do not need to shrink from our desire to be close. We need make no apologies for wanting to have someone to laugh with, share our day, and make fun and exciting plans with. The Creator Himself designed us to be in an intimate, joyful marriage.

Fear of Intimacy

In spite of our yearning to be close to others, and in spite of our God-given need for this closeness, we often create numerous barriers to prevent it from happening. At the very least, we maneuver ourselves so that intimacy does not develop with more intensity than we are comfortable with. At the most, we find ways to sabotage it with regularity.

Why is intimacy so frightening? Rooted in each of us is the prideful desire to be perfect. We do not relish sharing our imperfections with others. If I reveal to you who I am—warts and all—you will know the real me. Yikes! This can be scary stuff. Most relationships are a series of maneuvers designed to move us closer to or away from others, depending on our needs at the moment. Harriet Goldhor Lerner, in her book *The Dance of Intimacy,* says that moving back and forth in a relationship is natural.

> Most of us rely on some form of distancing as a primary way to manage intensity in key relationships…Distancing is a useful way to manage intensity when it moves us from a situation of high reactivity and allows us to get calm enough to reflect, plan, and generate new options for our behavior. Often, however, we rely on distance and a cutoff to exit permanently (emotionally or physically) from a significant relationship without really addressing the issues and problems.[4]

The implication is that we all must decide for ourselves what level of intimacy we are comfortable with—and how we can best attain it. What is comfortable for one person may be unbearable for another. While some may deeply desire intimacy, others prefer something less intense.

For example, most of us have to work out how close we will live to our parents. Some will choose to live minutes away and may call on a daily basis to stay intimately connected. Others would find this suffocating. They will choose to live hours away and contact their parents once every few weeks to catch up on the latest news. Still others will live three times zones away and may only talk to their parents once or twice a year. As you can see, this is a highly personal matter.

Married couples also need to manage an appropriate amount of distance. Distance can be a good thing if we manage it properly and if it's not rooted in fear. Couples need to talk about having times of solitude and respite alone so that they can come back together ready for contact. They may also need to talk about how frightening intimacy is for them.

Working Out the Dance

Working out the dance of intimacy is one thing with our parents, but it is something else with our spouses. We are pretty clear about needing some space from our parents; we are often less conscious of our need for balance between closeness and space where our spouses are concerned. After we have said "I do," we struggle to move to the next level, one where we are comfortable with both our individuality and our commitment to our mate.

Finding a way to identify our intimacy needs and then meeting them can be a huge challenge. Creating a relationship in which we can discuss these issues is a critical beginning. Let's consider a few additional practical steps.

Take the Risk

The first step in moving closer to your mate is simply making the decision to do so. This is a huge stride. Once you decide that you want to be more transparent, you will make decisions to reveal yourself more to your mate.

To reap the benefits of intimacy means you must first take the risk of being seen. You risk being shamed, ridiculed, or misunderstood by your spouse, though I certainly hope this will not happen. Instead, I hope you will talk to your spouse about taking these steps toward greater intimacy and agree to honor this sacred trust—sharing without shame.

One of the first steps for Trudy in dealing with her lifeless marriage was to take the risk of being honest with her husband. She had to approach him and tell him that their marriage was dull. She had to risk feeling foolish and perhaps even ridiculed for her desire for greater closeness. Until she did this, nothing would change.

So, like Trudy, prepare yourself for taking the risk of getting close to your spouse again. Brace yourself for the vulnerability the risk demands.

Refocus

Many couples become distracted in the daily routine of life. I have talked to many women who would rather spend time with their children and involve themselves in their children's activities than honestly face the struggles in their marriage. They tried to talk to their husbands about this need for closeness and eventually felt rebuffed when the man did not figure things out on his own, so they turn their attentions to their children. This is not much different from men distracting themselves with sports or outdoor pursuits rather than honestly facing their frustrations on the home front.

Enhancing intimacy requires focus. As a magnifying glass concentrates light toward a single point, focus draws our energies in a clear direction. We take time to plan and prayerfully evaluate how to reenergize our marriages. We close the "back door"—the route that distracts us from the pain we feel from emptiness in marriage. We must face—again and again if necessary—the raw challenges of intimacy.

We must always have a personal plan for bringing excitement and energy into the marriage—those fun outings, private lunches, walks on the beach, afternoons at the symphony. Your list (or jar of surprise outings) will look different from mine, but it is just as important.

So let's get clear about the problem. You need to move other important issues to the side of your plate in order to have any hope of fine-tuning your marriage. Let's look at several key areas that need focus.

Give Up Secrets

Secrets poison relationships. You know the kind: hidden addictions, adulterous affairs, excessive spending. Sometimes the secrets are small, seemingly innocuous. More often, they start small and grow into infections that contaminate the marriage. Why are secrets so damaging?

Secrets are usually kept because they are inherently destructive. The alcoholic who has promised to quit but now hides his booze creates rage and distrust in the marriage. His wife doesn't know what to believe. He swears he has quit and insists that the booze she has found in the basement is not even his, despite the absurdity of this statement. It is his brand, and he has lied about this before. She is beside herself with fear that he has relapsed and, even worse, that he will not seek help for his alcoholism.

Once discovered, secrets sow the seeds of distrust. Secrets say to the other partner, "I couldn't trust you to tell you straight out, so I hid this part of my life from you." Without a foundation of trust, relationships can never be healthy and satisfying.

So, even at the risk of anger and hurt, be honest. Get rid of secrets.

Tell your spouse those things you know you need to bring to the table of your marriage.

Be Generous in Love

Somewhere along the way, we have forgotten how to be romantic. We have forgotten the importance of kindling the fires of love once the honeymoon is over. We have decided that being generous in love was frivolous, unnecessary, a waste of time.

You know this attitude is both false and damaging. You can observe in your own marriage the difference between those times when you are romantic and generous with your love and those when you are too busy to bother with such things. When you are caring and romantic, your spouse responds in kind with affection. When you are stingy with your affections, when you are too preoccupied to shower your love on your spouse and family, you become detached, and your family responds in kind. This is how your emotional life can begin to wither and die.

Being generous with your love is critically important. Show that you care, every day and in every way you can think of. How about trying a few of the following ideas?

- Greet your spouse with a smile and "good morning" when you wake up.
- Say "I love you" every day.
- Offer to take turns making dinner.
- Take the initiative planning a date.
- Offer praise generously on your spouse's appearance.

Living in Love

Many things can create distance in a relationship. A marriage rarely grows stale for just one reason. But one thing is certain: A marriage filled with pleasant, sensuous surprises—where no one takes the other for granted—enjoys a degree of immunity against the ravages of boredom and detachment. An act of attentiveness can melt away the distance in an instant.

Think about it. When was the last time you came home to a candlelight dinner, fresh flowers, and a little Sinatra in the background? When was the last time you thought about creating a magical evening or weekend for your spouse? When was the last time you booked a night away at a bed-and-breakfast overlooking the water?

Alexandra Stoddard, in her book *Living in Love,* tells of the early days with her husband, Peter. Because both been married before, they had cautiously waited several years before considering marrying again. But the two became friends and that friendship eventually turned to love.

If you are familiar with Alexandra Stoddard, you know she is trained as an interior designer and writer. You know she lives life fully and gives of herself completely in her relationships. She eloquently shares the details of her ongoing love affair with Peter.

She tells of awakening together and sharing breakfast on their sun-soaked patio. They converse freely about the blessings of nature in evidence around their home, but more importantly, they openly and unabashedly display their affection for one another. They seem to bask in one another's delight in the other.

> Before he sits down to continue his breakfast, Peter walks to the edge of the terrace, plucks a pink hibiscus, and brings it over to put in my hair. He takes another bite of his honey-soaked muffin...Here on this terrace lingering over coffee, I daydream about our lifetime of love together. I think about all we have been through, how much I'm

looking forward to the surprises of the future. I think about love.[5]

Many would reject Stoddard's writing, calling her a hopeless, syrupy romantic (to which she might give assent), but I find myself drawn to it. I have many of her books, and I invariably smile when I imagine her and Peter sharing breakfast, their hopes and concerns for the day, and their devotion for one another.

Alexandra and Peter are public about the fact that this is her second marriage and his third. Although they do not share the details of their earlier marriages, they seem to be taking extra precautions to keep the intimacy alive and well in this one. They have seen and experienced the sweetness of love and watched it fade over time. Do you suppose they are more determined to keep the love fresh this time around? Might they now be willing to be gleefully in love? They are willing to share their affections freely and make surprise an essential element in their relationship. Could we possibly talk about our mates the way Alexandra describes Peter?

> He clicks his fingers and taps his toes. He shoots the waves and splashes with me in the water. He whistles, makes bird calls, dances for joy, skips upstairs, singing "Hey, ho." He doesn't need anything to be happy about, he's so filled with gratitude to be living in love. What a transcendent, effervescent blessing to live in love with such a vital spirit.[6]

In a recent conversation, a woman told me how she had begun the practice of paying more attention to her husband's positive attributes rather than dwelling on his negatives. She was amazed at the results of this simple exercise. She smiled as she recalled some of the quirks she still found endearing. Instead of focusing on his habits that annoyed her, she shifted her focus and was pleased to find her affections for him returning.

The Power of Apology

Contrition is an extremely powerful tool in maintaining a healthy relationship. Why we apologize so rarely is beyond me—other than the obvious: To apologize and admit fault renders the almighty ego vulnerable.

Apologies are essential for keeping love strong. Why? Because we will always make mistakes that threaten the bond of intimacy. This is part of being human. We will hurt each other's feelings during times of insensitivity and anger, and apologies are a way to mend fences. Telling your mate that you are sorry for harming him or her can be a powerful path back to trust and intimacy. Something about the words "I'm sorry" is tremendously disarming.

"I'm sorry" is an excellent start, but the better apology says more. To truly mend the brokenness in the relationship, we go further:

- We admit regret for our actions.
- We admit to the specifics of what we've done wrong.
- We admit the impact of our actions on our partner.
- We admit responsibility for the wrongdoing.
- We admit willingness to remedy the wrong—including offering restitution.

To withhold an apology is a serious and potentially damaging mistake, in spite of the ego's protests to the contrary. When you know that you have harmed your spouse and yet are too proud to apologize, you drive a stake between the two of you. Your partner's wound festers for want of an apology.

Soften your heart and apologize for the things that you know you have done wrong. Don't wait for your partner to apologize for his or her actions; take the initiative and apologize for the harm you have done—and then watch the powerful effects of that apology.

The apologies we offer our spouses and others are also offerings we can give to God. He wants us to come with our heartfelt remorse for sinful actions, and this is a way to renew our relationship to Him.

Forgiving Yourself and Others

Having done your work of apologizing, you must now do the work of forgiving yourself. In fact, until you can at least partially forgive yourself, you will be too focused on your needs to focus effectively on your mate. Forgiving yourself clears the way for you to truly empathize with your partner and make the appropriate apology.

In my counseling work, I find that forgiving ourselves is as difficult a task as forgiving others. We tend to place more emphasis on forgiving others—for those grudges are more obvious—but forgiving ourselves is at least as arduous a challenge.

At a workshop I attended several years ago, we received an assignment to cut out different pieces from magazines, creating a mosaic that depicted the life we wanted in the future. This seemed like a simple assignment, and I began cutting out pictures of sailboats, water, mountains, as well as words like *reflection, inspiration,* and *imagine,* which are all symbolic of important parts of my life.

We busied ourselves with our projects, gathering fitting words and pictures while throwing away the scrap pieces. At the end of the project, as the other participants and I sat admiring our work, the leader asked a startling question:

"What have you done with the extra scraps of paper?"

"Well, we threw them away, of course," we responded.

The leader looked piercingly at us for a moment. Then she spoke softly.

"Sometimes the extra pieces of our lives, the things we call scraps or mistakes, are actually important components. We are too quick to throw them away—to label them as trash. They can help create the texture that makes our lives interesting and uniquely ours."

I have never forgotten that illustration. When I get discouraged about all the mistakes in my life and walk carefully with others through the debris of their difficulties, I am soothed by Paul's words: "And we know that in all things [mistakes, blunders, goof-ups and outright catastrophes that we desperately want to forget!] God works for the good of those who love him, who have been called according to his purpose" (Romans 8:28).

Brennan Manning, in his wonderful book *The Ragamuffin Gospel*, speaks to all of us with crooked halos. He reminds us that we are prodigals desiring the loving embrace of the father as we return, again and again, from our egocentric ways. In the context of our weary, wounded worlds, Manning focuses on Jesus' instruction to love "the least of these." Manning wonders, might the least of these, at times, be you and me?

But when we make a mistake, can we really own up to it, make amends for it, and then offer grace to ourselves? Do you beat yourself up with questions that only serve to tear apart your esteem? Do you obsess, as I do at times, about those occasions when you could have been more loving as a husband? Do you wonder what you might have done as a parent to create a more responsible child? Do you question what you might have done to cause your spouse to betray you or tune you out?

We often need to remind ourselves of Jesus' words to love our neighbor *as* we love ourselves—not *instead* of loving ourselves.

The Scriptures have much to say on this topic of forgiving others. As always, Jesus has direct and valuable advice for us.

I refer again to Jesus' words concerning forgiveness. In the Lord's Prayer, He not only teaches us to pray but encourages us to ask for forgiveness as we have forgiven others their sins against us. He goes on to say, "For if you forgive men when they sin against you, your heavenly Father will also forgive you. But if you do not forgive men their sins, your Father will not forgive your sins" (Matthew 6:14-15).

Certainly, we do not want to trifle with that admonition. We must see the issue of forgiving others as a mandate, not as optional. We cannot take lightly Jesus' directives to love our neighbors and to "Do to others as you would have them do to you" (Luke 6:31). We are told that we must forgive, forgive, and forgive again (Matthew 18:21-22).

Forgive yourself. Forgive others. This will allow you to rebuild any broken bridges to intimacy.

Spiritual Intimacy

We can express intimacy in many ways. Most of us are quick to recognize physical and emotional intimacy—or the lack of it—in our relationships, but we are not as quick to think and talk about spiritual intimacy.

Author and theologian Henri Nouwen, in his book *Lifesigns,* states, "The life, death, and resurrection of Jesus manifest to us the full intimacy of this divine embrace. He lived our lives, died our deaths, and lifted all of us up into his glory. There is no suffering he has not suffered in the agony of Jesus on the cross, no human joy that has not been celebrated by Jesus in his resurrection to new life."

Nouwen believes that intimacy with Jesus demands that we are intimate with others. "We cannot live in intimate communion with Jesus without being sent to our brothers and sisters who belong to that same humanity that Jesus has accepted as his own. Thus intimacy manifests itself as solidarity, and solidarity as intimacy."[7]

Nouwen is not naive. He recognizes that we are generally a fragmented people. But he challenges us to develop new eyes and new ears to hear the truth of our unity. He challenges us to be people whose prayer is deeper and, therefore, whose love and acceptance are deeper. "God wants to open our eyes so that we can see that we belong together in the embrace of God's perfect love."[8]

As I consider the importance of intimacy, I wonder about Trudy, the caller who found herself and her husband living separate lives in the same home. While clearly discouraged, she offered that she was a Christian and longed for intimacy with her husband again. She shared that her husband was also a Christian. Although we don't know what has happened to them, we can be confident that she is praying for their marriage and is ready to talk earnestly with him about broaching the distance in their marriage. She is ready to refocus her life on her marriage, give up her secrets, and risk getting close to him. She is committed to bathing her efforts in prayer, seeking God to first change her heart and then her husband's.

Intimacy can only be created when we have yielded our hearts to Jesus. I used to believe otherwise. I thought I could will myself to be more loving. If I practiced myriad techniques, perhaps I could be a perfectly loving and accepting man.

Having tripped on those words and that attitude a thousand times, I am ready to surrender: I will truly love only to the extent that I am willing to give my heart over to the loving embrace of God. Only then will I find the sweetness of true intimacy with others.

Chapter Eleven

Finding the Strength and Ability to Change

Change is not merely necessary to life. It is life.
—ALVIN TOFFLER

———— 〰 ————

Old joke: How many psychologists does it take to change
a light bulb?
Answer: Only one, but the light bulb really has to commit
itself to the change.

Sometimes I consider the magnitude of my profession. Some people consider psychologists to be confessor-priests, healer-physicians, or magicians. Indeed, our task can be daunting. People come to our doors because they hurt and want to feel better. They look to us for answers. They are afraid that they cannot change, that they will change too dramatically, or that the price for change will be too high.

As I reflect upon my role, I think about the changes I have experienced since I entered the field as a wide-eyed, Pollyannaish student many years ago. How the senior psychologists must have chuckled at my youthful enthusiasm. How they must have smirked when I smugly announced that I could treat anyone successfully in my groups on the Psychiatric Unit of Providence Hospital in Portland, Oregon.

They must have sat back and said, "Let him go. He'll learn in time." *How difficult could change be?* I mused back then. If the patient was willing, the cure could not be far behind.

Giddy with the power that accompanied working on this unit, dressed in a crisp, white lab coat that distanced me from the patients, I decided that the master's degree I was pursuing would not be enough. I wanted more training so that I could be even more effective. In truth, I suppose I just wanted more power. I wanted more patients, interns, and staff to look to me for answers. I wanted everyone to call me Doctor Hawkins.

Of course, the senior psychologists and psychiatrists were right. I couldn't treat everyone effectively in my groups. Many who came to the unit in crisis became stabilized, only to return to the same lives they left, and then back to the unit six months later, basically unchanged. Reality began to sink in for me.

Now, some 30 years later, with thousands of clinical hours under my belt, I am less giddy and far more realistic. The doctorate has been helpful, but it has provided no panacea for assisting people through the portals of change. My work is sobering. I still dispense hope, but it is liberally seasoned with reason. I understand that my suggestions and interventions can only go so far. The sky is no longer the limit. Silent prayers for help are more common in the therapeutic hour now.

What have I learned through years of working with anguished souls? What have I seen again and again when working with couples who, like helpless observers, continue to make one mistake after another? What has time taught me about the prospect of change?

What I have learned is this: Change is far more difficult than we imagine. In large part, this is because the self or ego can only accomplish so much. More than cosmetic and transitory change, we need inner transformation, and this comes from surrendering our hearts to Jesus Christ. When we give ourselves over to the changing power of Christ, all things become possible.

The Resistant Ego

To speak out against the ego seems almost blasphemous for a psychologist. After all, so much of our work has to do with strengthening the powers of the ego—helping it solve problems, make rational decisions, and "grow up." A strong ego is crucial to an individual's wholeness and healthy functioning.

Problems arise, however, when the ego becomes too powerful, as mine was when I was a student. We so easily choose the dangerous path of building up false selves. When this happens, we begin to believe we have more power than we actually have. We begin to believe we are more important than we actually are. Sadly, the more we identify with these false selves—these all-important, all-knowing personas—the greater our troubles become. The kingdoms we build for ourselves isolate us from opportunities for true change.

I recently counseled a man who had lost his temper over something incredibly trivial—his wife had accidentally burned his steak. He chided her for "not being able to cook properly." He had looked forward to a delicious, medium-rare steak, and when things did not go as he had planned, he flew into a brief but intimidating rage. His wife was frightened, hurt, and angered by his childish outburst.

As I listened to him and his wife, he rigidly stuck to his position that he should not have to apologize. "It made me mad. That's all. I don't see why I should have to say I'm sorry when she was the one who burned the steak. Besides, the whole thing was over in a few minutes. I'm no different from most men—I blow up and then it's over. I don't mean anything by it. I don't want her upset. She needs to let it go."

"But it doesn't seem to be over for her," I said. "She has to live with the effects of your anger."

"Well, that's just the way I am. It shouldn't be any big deal." He paused for a moment, looked down, and said, "I suppose I shouldn't lose control, but that's what guys do. Everybody at the mill talks the way I talk. That's just the way things are."

And so this man chose to live with his hardened heart. He seems to have a faint glimpse that he is too full of himself. He seems to want a better marriage—just as long as he doesn't have to change. He has learned to identify with his image of the quick-tempered man and soothes his conscience by telling himself that other men behave just as he does.

In this example, we witness the dark side of the ego. We see its pettiness and self-serving approach to living. Yet each of us can identify with this type of behavior.

Perhaps we are not "exploders" like the man with the burned steak. Perhaps we respond passive-aggressively and refuse to speak. Or perhaps we storm out of the room when angry. The bottom line is that our egos are alive and well, and they most certainly are responsible for causing problems in our relationships.

Ego does not give in to change easily. In fact, this self-protective, tyrannical ruler has trouble allowing itself to relinquish power or to submit to change. For the ego to listen to the gentle voice of reason would be equivalent to a king stepping off the throne and allowing the servants to rule the kingdom.

I am reminded of Paul's words: "Those who let themselves be controlled by their lower natures live only to please themselves, but those who follow after the Holy Spirit find themselves doing what pleases God" (Romans 8:8 TLB).

The Caterpillar

I was terribly disconcerted to discover that people are fickle about change. I was ready to be a midwife for damaged souls who supposedly wanted a healthier life. I was anxious to greet people at the door of my office with visions of them leaving with new skills and new attitudes. I imagined that people would be willing to do anything to attain a healthier life.

What I discovered differed markedly from what I had imagined. People do desperately long for new lives, but they cling tenaciously to their old ones. They say they want renewal, but they balk if the price seems too high. Suddenly, the old life doesn't look so bad after all.

Some people seem to believe that cosmetic change—like the stomach-staple as a solution for weight loss—is an adequate response to marital problems. "You want me to come to marriage counseling for *how long?*" they ask, surprised when they learn that years of problems cannot be cured in a single session. Those who want change at all want it fast. Their impatience is another version of the American obsession with instant gratification.

Sue Monk Kidd, in her compelling book *When the Heart Waits*, walks us metaphorically through the changes in the life of the caterpillar. She explains that the caterpillar subjects itself not just to cosmetic change but to complete transformation. No dab of rouge or eye shadow here. A complete makeover.

Consider the caterpillar. It willingly enters the cocoon, surely a dark and lonely place. There, during the cold of winter, something more than change happens. Death occurs. The caterpillar subjects itself to the elements of metamorphosis—radical transformation. But first the old nature must die. "Unless a kernel of wheat falls to the ground and dies, it remains only a single seed" (John 12:24).

Kidd weaves the story of the caterpillar—chrysalis to butterfly. She shares the value of this miraculous lesson from nature. During the long, slow winter nights, when nothing seems to be happening, when all that is present seems to be without life, a yeasting process is taking place. Like the work of the Spirit on our inner nature, something deep, abiding, and life-changing is transpiring. True, deep, inner transformation does not occur without the necessary time and ingredients. Anything less will inevitably lead to disappointment.

"Transformations come only as we go the long way round," Kidd writes, "only as we're willing to walk a different, longer, more arduous, more inward, more prayerful route. When you wait, you're deliberately choosing to take the long way, to go eight blocks instead of four, trusting that there's a transforming discovery lying pooled along the way."[1]

People want to short-circuit this process. We want quick-change artistry.

Many years ago I raised chickens. At one point, I decided to incubate eggs and raise my own chicks. The project was very exciting for me. I became eager during the weeks of incubation. I imagined the embryonic life inside the dark shells and found myself exhilarated when new life began to emerge.

In fact, as the births were underway, I was so worried that the chicks would have difficulty pecking their way out of their shells that I decided to lend a helping hand. I took a knife and peeled away the brittle shell and tissue-membrane and waited for the chicks to spring forth. To my horror, every chick died. Moments before, tiny beaks had poked their way into a new world. Now only damp, lifeless bodies remained.

I began to weep when I realized what I had done. I had tended to these young chicks, from conception to birth, only to watch them die as a result of my impatience. I did not have the self-discipline to let them complete their transformation process.

Henry David Thoreau, America's solitary walker, considers the notion of patience and real change. "You think I am impoverishing myself by withdrawing from men, but in my solitude I have woven for myself a silken web or chrysalis, and nymph-like shall ere long burst forth a more perfect creature."[2]

Surrender

If we listen to Kidd, Thoreau, and, of course, the Scriptures, we must wrestle with the idea of patient, in-depth change. If we really want to become different people, we must first invite the Holy Spirit into our personal chrysalis.

But, as much as we may want to change and stop making those dreadful mistakes that hamper our marriages, change will not happen as long as we cling to our ego-entrusted way of doing things. As a therapist, I am painfully aware of the limits to how much we can change ourselves.

Those who have had success in 12-step programs will tell you that every moment of peace from their alcoholism, drug addiction, or codependency comes when they surrender their self-will to their higher power—God. They know that capitulation is the key.

Change occurs as we relinquish our old life, our old ways of thinking and behaving, to the renewing life of Christ. As we subject ourselves to His will, our will is remade. This leads to a changed heart and the ability to truly live out the transformations I have talked about in this book.

Listen to Kidd talk about the process of letting go.

> We have within us a deep longing to grow and become a new creature, but we possess an equally strong compulsion to remain the same—to burrow down in our safe, secure places...Shifting from our self-centered focus to a more God-centered focus is terribly hard. I think we've gone wrong by assuming that such a radical movement can be achieved simply by setting our jaw and saying one or two prayers of relinquishment. Letting go isn't one step but many. It's a winding, spiraling process that happens on deep levels. And we must begin at the beginning: by confronting our ambivalence.[3]

But is our desire to change as powerful as our egotistical belief in self-reliance? Surrender is so un-American. "Let go? No way! I will fight and kick and try and try again. I will not quit. I will not surrender."

Can't you hear us raising our voices in a unified chant? "We can win. We will persist. We will never give up. We will overcome—and we will do so on our own." Amidst all of this kicking and screaming, we are unwilling to bow our heads and, in sweet surrender, ask God to heal our hearts. And God weeps.

Richard Bode, in his book *First You Have to Row a Little Boat*, shares his personal battle with surrender and eventual acceptance of chrysalis-living. He tells of ignoring painful symptoms in the hope that his physical problem might go away.

"I had been forcing my legs to carry my body in a direction it didn't want to go, and now, no longer able to bear the awesome burden, my right hip joint had rebelled. I awoke from the anesthesia [from surgery] in a plaster body cast that extended from my chest to my toes."[4]

His nurse helps him with the physical and emotional aspects of his ordeal. "Well, there you are, safe and sound inside your cocoon," she says. "Who do you think you'll be when you emerge?"

Trapped in his motionless world, Bode had no option but to reflect on his life. Sometimes life—as revealed through forces God has set in motion—will compel us to surrender in spite of our will.

"Day after day," Bode writes, "as I lay in my enforced idleness, I thought deeply about who I was, where I came from, and what I wanted to be. What I had lost in physical motion I had gained in insight, which is movement of another kind. I learned the interior life was as rewarding as the exterior life and that my richest moments occurred when I was absolutely still."[5]

Inside-Out Change

The story of the caterpillar's journey has many applications.

Perhaps most amazing is when the caterpillar—ready to be changed from the inside out—surrenders its life to the dark, lonely reaches of the chrysalis.

Conversely, most of us want to be changed from the outside in. We either want cosmetic changes to remedy our problems, or worse, we want our environment to change so that we can feel better.

Gary is a fairly typical client. A middle-aged alcoholic, prone to relapse, he was mired in a miserable marriage and a miserable job. Not surprisingly, he was feeling miserable to boot. When he came to see me, he was filled with anger and resentment. He believed the answer was for his wife of 20 years to change. She had recently left him and was deliberating about whether or not to make the arrangement permanent. According to Gary, she insisted that he receive treatment before she would return home.

You might assume Gary would quickly surrender and seek treatment under these circumstances, but his will was formidable, despite the absurdity of his rationale. During the first several sessions Gary clearly stated that he saw no reason to alter his behavior. He wanted to turn his wife into the loving, doting mother he never had. He wanted her to accept him the way he was. He insisted that he only relapsed into binge drinking every six months or so. What was the big deal? In fact, he blamed the majority of their problems on her, creatively rationalizing and minimizing his own role in these issues.

Although I was encouraged because Gary had agreed to attend counseling, he had no real desire to change from the inside out. He expected that if he offered his wife the promise that he would quit binge drinking, she would come back to him. He had sent her a card telling her how much he loved her. He thought that if he offered her a few crumbs they would taste like a gourmet meal.

His wife was smarter than that. She had been through this scenario numerous times. She insisted he enter treatment and change the lifestyle that was contributing to his relapses. Meanwhile, he wanted her to be content with half-measures.

I am no longer a rookie. I don't have a cure-all. I understand that Gary will linger in his malaise until he figures out that self-serving, superficial changes will not bring his wife back—nor will they address his alcoholism.

It is intriguing to watch the cosmetic surgery industry, which we Americans support by spending millions of dollars annually to bolster our outward appearances. Of course, our real desire is to somehow improve our flagging sense of self-esteem. I must admit that I am tempted by the alluring ads that tout "body beautiful." The crow's feet have no business at the corners of my eyes. I've read about superwhoopee ways to take ten years off my appearance with a nip here and a tuck there. And if surgery isn't your thing, you can choose from an assortment of face creams, body oils, laser treatments for facial resurfacing and hair removal, and let's not forget the real deal—spa treatments guaranteed to make you feel youthful again. Of course, at 50-something, I am taking notice.

I am not categorically opposed to these treatments. My only hope is that we will keep these things in perspective. Removing the lines and wrinkles will not make you whole, nor will they wipe away the mistakes you are making in your marriage. A straighter nose or stronger chin will not change how you talk to your husband when he annoys you. Those alterations must be made from the inside out. They require that you alter your character.

But we have mixed feelings about making changes from the inside out. Not only do we have ambivalence about surrender, we have ambivalence about owning our mistakes. Like the client who threw a temper tantrum because his steak was overcooked and then refused to humble himself and admit his guilt, most of us offer only tepid apologies at best. We tender excuses for our behaviors; we rationalize, minimize, and justify our actions. Anything to keep us from feeling bad. Then we grit our teeth and wait for our spouses to arrive with the olive branch before we will admit any semblance of wrong.

In order for meaningful change to occur, we must soften our hearts. And for that to take place, we must be willing to let God work on us from the inside out.

Paul says to the Corinthians: "Now I am happy, not because you were made sorry, but because your sorrow led you to repentance" (2 Corinthians 7:9).

Here is the beauty of the gospel at work—sorrow leading to repentance. Sorrow that comes from devouring the living Word that is active and sharper than a two-edged sword (Hebrews 4:12). Sorrow that comes from a heart touched by the Holy Spirit dwelling within the believer. This is how real change takes place. Nothing cosmetic will ever be effective. Nothing superficial will result in consequential change. Sorrow leads a person to turn 180 degrees and move in an entirely new direction.

Repentance

Repentance is not a word we use every day, but it is an important one nonetheless. Repentance has to do with change from the inside out.

Caterpillar-to-chrysalis-to-butterfly change.

Heart change.

The Greek word for repentance is *metanoeo*, which literally means "a change of mind and purpose in life, to which remission of sin is promised."[6] So repenting of the mistakes we've talked about in this book means not only avoiding the surface behaviors that lead to the mistakes, but also being concerned with heart attitudes that give way to new behaviors. Repentance equates to heart surgery.

What are the qualities of the repentant heart?

- The repentant heart feels godly sorrow and an understanding of the wrongfulness of our behavior.

- The repentant heart understands that the wrong goes against God as well as against others. We grieve God when we violate His standards.

- The repentant heart is a humble heart, recognizing that we are no better than others and are as inclined to make mistakes as anyone else.

- The repentant heart forgives, understanding that we too are capable of hurtful actions and need forgiveness.

- The repentant heart takes complete responsibility for our part in the wrong. We consider how our actions have hurt others.

- The repentant heart is willing to take whatever steps are necessary to remedy the wrong. We will seek ways to make peace in the broken relationship.

- The repentant heart will guard the heart in the future, minimizing the risk of making the same mistake again.

- The repentant heart is willing to be held accountable for corrective change. We maintain our lives as "open books" so others can see into our lives and actions.

- The repentant heart is a reconciling heart, ready to establish peace again. We are quick to offer peace and reconciliation.

After having heart surgery, forgiveness is, thankfully, available to all. Striving for peaceful living, we realize that we will make mistakes. But with confession and repentance, the Scriptures tell us, those who long for Christ's peacefulness in their hearts experience no condemnation (Romans 8:33-34).

Nine Critical Mistakes

As I have illustrated in this book, *mistakes* are different from *critical mistakes*. Every couple makes garden-variety mistakes that have little impact on the integrity of the marriage. But our concern is with those that tear the very fabric of the relationship. Unless you address and remedy these mistakes, your marriage is headed for real trouble.

Let's summarize again the mistakes we have addressed in this book, and see how surrendering to the life-changing power of God can help us solve these problems.

- *Don't push the plunger.* When frustrated, we too often send our discussions in a downward, blaming, lose-lose spiral. The transformed heart will not be so easily frustrated because it is not so attached to outcomes. The fruit of the transformed heart is a love that does not seek its own way (1 Corinthians 13:5).

- *Stop whistling Dixie.* Rather than avoid the tough issues in marriage, the transformed heart is willing to speak honestly with others. Buoyed by a close relationship with Christ, we are able to "speak the truth in love" and understand that truth will set us free. The Psalmist says, "I do not hide your righteousness in my heart; I speak of your faithfulness and salvation. I do not conceal your love and your truth from the great assembly" (Psalm 40:10).

- *Stop speaking Greek.* Instead of using obscure, distracting language as a way to avoid addressing the real issues, the transformed heart is willing to engage in straight talk. We learn the importance of asking for what we need and expressing our feelings openly and honestly.

- *Stop playing God.* Pontificating, preaching, labeling, or telling your partner how it is or what he or she needs to do doesn't help. In fact, criticizing or parenting a partner only creates resentment. The transformed heart is a humble heart. Knowing that we are all sinners, we accept that we have no right to preach to others.

- *Stop kicking a dead horse.* Dragging out subjects that we have discussed over and over again only breeds hostility. The transformed heart refuses to rehearse resentments or make mountains out of molehills. Instead, it chooses to let go of old wounds, allowing us to see our partners as God sees them—through eyes of love.

- *Stop living in the trenches.* The transformed heart loosens the chains of routine and familiarity. As a result, we will choose to champion our mates. We practice seeing the best in our partners, cheering them on to be what they want to be. We understand the importance of saying only what is good and helpful (Ephesians 4:29).

- *Stop using that untamed tongue.* Bitter, angry words have no place in a relationship. The transformed heart understands the lasting impact harsh words have on marriage and knows how to set limits on vitriolic exchanges.

- *Stop living behind paper fences.* The transformed heart knows the importance of individuality in marriage and learns to build firm, appropriate boundaries. This includes a clear definition of what we will and will not tolerate.

- *Stop being distant.* The transformed heart is willing to allow us to get close to our mate. We are willing to explore ways of practicing the fine art of intimacy—*into-me-see.* We are able to step forward and be vulnerable.

The transformed heart knows the truth about the limitations on what we can change with our own strength. We need God to alter our hearts because change from the inside out is our truest and most lasting source of transformation.

Sacrificial Love

Love requires a certain amount of sacrifice. In fact, the greater the sacrifice, the deeper the love. Conversely, the more the commanding, grabbing, manipulative ego gets involved, the more complicated your love life becomes. But the more we give of ourselves, our *true* selves, the more we experience the joys of love. Daphne Rose Kingma, author of *The Future of Love*, discusses generosity as a necessary ingredient in sacrificial love.

> It is in giving with no ulterior motive, expecting nothing in return. We often think that generosity is a consequence, that because life or a certain person has been generous with us, we can now be generous in return. Since our own cup is filled to overflowing we can give of the excess. Finally, because we have so much, we figure that giving won't hurt. But true generosity is just plain giving all the time, as if we were a fountain, a river, an ocean, as if there were no end to what we have to give, as if we had nothing to consider but giving itself.[7]

Kingma goes on to describe how most relationships work: You give to me and then I'll give to you. Tit for tat. You forgive me and then perhaps I will forgive you. If you are rude to me, then I'll be rude to you. But in the new paradigm, in the model of sacrificial love most of us know about but fear, "we can be generous because we know that there are no insatiable needs and there is nothing to protect...We can give not only our material possessions but our words, our bodies, our insights, our time, our money, our empathy, our listening, and our compassion."[8]

If this counsel sounds troublesome to you, join the crowd. Too often, I live in a tit-for-tat world. I certainly aspire to grander things, but too often I fail to attain them. I recognize my dilemma. I am living with a natural worldview rather than the view from the transformed heart. I succumb easily to this worldview that says I must win in order to attain more, that I must be first in order to not lose out. I slip too quickly into believing I must always guard myself from being hurt rather than losing my life for the sake of others. The world of the transformed heart is a bit risky.

The apostle Paul is a superior teacher about generous love. In 2 Corinthians 9:6-7 Paul instructs us, "Whoever sows sparingly will also reap sparingly, and whoever sows generously will reap generously. Each man should give what he has decided in his heart to give, not reluctantly or under compulsion, for God loves a cheerful giver."

Although this passage refers to material things, it certainly applies to generous acts of love. Paul's numerous letters are filled with the implication that we are to love others freely and abundantly—because of God's love for us.

John Piper, in his book *Desiring God,* says, "Love is the overflow of joy in God that gladly meets the needs of others. It is the impulse of the fountain to overflow. It originates in the grace of God, which overflows freely because it delights to fill the empty. Love shares the nature of that grace because it too delights to overflow freely to meet the needs of others."[9]

Piper challenges the soft Christian. Love is not cheap or easy. Nor should it be. It is not based on whether I feel like behaving in a loving manner. Rather, Piper tells us, "Love is costly. It always involves some kind of self-denial. It often demands suffering...The greatest labor of love that ever happened was possible because Jesus pursued the greatest imaginable joy, namely, the joy of being exalted to God's right hand in the assembly of a redeemed people."[10]

Both Jesus and Paul would tell us the same thing: We are to love freely because we have been loved freely. We are to let the truths of God's love sink into the deepest parts of us so that the grace we have received will spill out of us like an overflowing fountain that cannot help but release more love. Transformed, like the caterpillar, from the inside out, we become new creatures who find joy in giving joy to others.

So, what about critical mistakes? Will a transformed heart cause them to cease? No. We will always be human. But we will make fewer mistakes, and when we do make mistakes, we will feel regret and make amends quickly. Transformed hearts that have the markings of generosity, humility, peacefulness, and love will govern our lives and our marriages. These qualities will transform us and our relationships with others.

Take the Fire

Now it is time for you to take what you have learned from this book and apply it to your marriage and other relationships. You will need all of your skills, tenacity, inner strength, and—most importantly—the blazing empowerment provided by the Holy Spirit.

You cannot succeed alone. Difficult as it is to accept, you cannot succeed on your own strength and ability regardless of your level of education or years of marriage or good intentions. There are no quick fixes. You need all the skills this book has to offer, as well as the transformative power of Jesus. With that, all things are possible.

And more than anything, we first need the fire of passion and the fire of the Holy Spirit in order to set us on the path toward meaningful change. So, as you move forward in your marriage…

Take the fire!

Notes

Chapter 1—Learning from Our Mistakes

1. Charles Manz, *The Power of Failure* (San Francisco: Berrett-Koehler Publishers, Inc., 2002), 78.

Chapter 2—Stop Pushing the Plunger

1. Harville Hendrix, *Getting the Love You Want* (New York: Owl Books, 2001).

2. James Creighton, *How Loving Couples Fight* (Fairfield, CN: Aslan Publishing, 1990), 43.

3. James Creighton, *Don't Go Away Mad* (New York: Doubleday, 1989), 143.

4. Creighton, *How Loving Couples Fight,* 236.

Chapter 3—Stop Whistling Dixie

1. Sam Keen, *To Love and Be Loved* (New York: Bantam Books, 1997), 132.

2. Sharon Wegscheider-Cruse, *Coupleship* (Deerfield Beach, FL: Health Communications, Inc., 1988), 11-12.

3. Harriet Lerner, *The Dance of Anger* (New York: HarperCollins, 1985), 97.

4. Barbara Sher, *It's Only Too Late If You Don't Start Now* (New York: Dell Publishing, 1998), 131.

5. Harriet Goldhor Lerner, *The Dance of Intimacy* (New York, Harper & Row Publishers, 1989), 126.

Chapter 4—Stop Speaking Greek

1. Susan Heitler and Abigail Hirsch, *The Power of Two Workbook* (Oakland: New Harbinger Publications, 2003), 47.

2. George Bach and Ronald Deutsch, *Stop! You're Driving Me Crazy* (New York: Berkeley Publishing Group, 1985).

3. John Bradshaw, *Bradshaw On: The Family* (Deerfield Beach, FL: Health Communications, 1988), 171.

4. Don Miguel Ruiz, *The Four Agreements* (San Rafael, CA: Amber-Allen Publishing, 1997), 26.

5. Scott Peck, *The Road Less Traveled* (New York: Simon and Schuster, 1978), 151-3.

6. Ibid., 71.

Chapter 5—Stop Playing God

1. John Gottman, *The Seven Principles for Making Marriage Work* (New York: Three Rivers Press, 1999), 27.

2. Ibid., 29.

3. Carmen Renee Berry and Tamara Traeder, *Girlfriends* (Berkeley, CA: Wildcat Canyon Press, 1995), 183.

4. Harriet Goldhor Lerner, *The Dance of Intimacy* (New York: Harper & Row Publishers, 1989), 102.

5. Stephanie Dowrick, *Forgiveness and Other Acts of Love* (New York: W.W. Norton & Company, 1997), 252.

6. Scott Peck, *The Road Less Traveled* (New York: Simon and Schuster, 1978), 160-61.

7. Kahlil Gibran, *The Prophet* (New York: Alfred A. Knopf, 1955), 15-16.

8. Peck, 168.

9. Anthony Storr, *Solitude* (New York: Ballantine Books, 1988), 62.

Chapter 6—Stop Kicking a Dead Horse

1. Robert Wicks, *Touching the Holy* (Notre Dame: Ave Maria Press, 1992), 130.

2. David Augsburger, *Caring Enough to Forgive* (Ventura, CA: Regal Books, 1981), 51.

3. Marshall Rosenberg, *Nonviolent Communication* (Encinitas, CA: PuddleDancer Press, 2003), 145.

4. Ibid., 143.

5. Augsburger, 52.

6. Brennan Manning, *The Ragamuffin Gospel* (Sisters, OR: Multnomah Press, 1990), 182.

Chapter 7—Stop Living in the Trenches

1. Rosamund Stone Zander and Benjamin Zander, *The Art of Possibility* (Boston: Harvard Business School Press, 1994), 31-32.

2. Ibid., 26.

3. Les Parrott and Leslie Parrott, *When Bad Things Happen to Good Marriages* (Grand Rapids, MI: Zondervan Publishing House, 2001), 79.

4. Gary Smalley and John Trent, *The Blessing* (New York: Pocket Books, 1986), 24.

Chapter 8—Stop Living with Paper Fences

1. David Hawkins, *When Pleasing Others Is Hurting You* (Eugene, OR: Harvest House Publishers, 2004), 20.

2. Henry Cloud and John Townsend, *Boundaries* (Grand Rapids: Zondervan Publishing House, 1992), 150.

3. Henry Cloud and John Townsend, *Boundaries in Marriage* (Grand Rapids: Zondervan Publishing House, 1999), 32.

4. Ibid.

Chapter 9—Stop Using That Untamed Tongue

1. Clifton Fadiman, ed., *The Little, Brown Book of Anecdotes* (New York: Little, Brown & Company, 1985), 362.

2. John Gottman, *The Seven Principles for Making Marriage Work* (New York: Three Rivers Press, 1999), 65.

3. Les Parrott and Leslie Parrott, *When Bad Things Happen to Good Marriages* (Grand Rapids, MI: Zondervan Publishing House, 2001), 161.

4. Emmett Fox, *The Sermon on the Mount* (New York: Harper & Brother Publishers, 1934), 22.

Chapter 10—Stop Being Distant

1. Janet Woititz, *Struggle for Intimacy* (Pompano Beach, FL: Health Communications, Inc., 1985), 20-21.

2. Jane Hansen, *Fashioned for Intimacy* (New York: Regal Books, 1997), 52-53.

3. Ibid., 54.

4. Harriet Goldhor Lerner, *The Dance of Intimacy* (New York: Harper & Row Publishers, 1989), 54.

5. Alexandra Stoddard, *Living in Love* (New York: William Morrow & Company, 1997), 228.

6. Ibid., 229.

7. Henri Nouwen, *Lifesigns* (New York: Doubleday, 1986), 44.

8. Ibid., 46.

Chapter 11—Finding the Strength and Ability to Change

1. Sue Monk Kidd, *When the Heart Waits* (San Francisco: HarperSanFrancisco, 1990), 19.

2. Quoted by Robert Bly, *The Winged Life: The Poetic Voice of Henry David Thoreau* (San Francisco: Sierra Club Books, 1986), 58.

3. Kidd, 102.

4. Richard Bode, *First You Have to Row a Little Boat* (New York: Warner Books, 1993), 78.

5. Ibid., 79.

6. *Easton's 1897 Bible Dictionary.* Accessed online at www.dictionary.com.

7. Daphne Rose Kingma, *The Future of Love* (New York: Doubleday, 1998), 173.

8. Ibid.

9. John Piper, *Desiring God* (Sisters, OR: Multnomah Publishing, 1986), 123.

10. Ibid., 132.

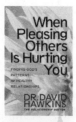